# GROUNDED

# GROUNDED

## LEADING YOUR
### *Life with Intention*

*Nancy M. Dahl*

MCP Books, Maitland, FL

MCP Books
2301 Lucien Way #415
Maitland, FL 32751
407-339-4217
www.millcitypress.net

ISBN-13: 978-1-54561-033-6

LCCN: 2016914771

Distributed by Itasca Books

Edited by: Tammie Lynn & Wendy Amundson

Printed in the United States of America

"GROUNDED illustrates the power of being a great student of life. "In school, you are taught a lesson and then given a test. In life, you are given a test that teaches you a lesson." (Tom Bodett) Nancy showcases the results of life tests so that both present and future leaders can learn how to take the road less traveled in our personal and professional lives."

-*Ertugrul Tuzcu*, Distinguished Service Professor, Opus College of Business, University of St. Thomas, former Retail Executive

"Nancy knows the power of conversation and human connection to inspire others to be their best at any age. The readers of GROUNDED will learn to lead happier and more productive lives. Nancy's self-deprecating style captures lessons learned in a way that benefits others and feels like she is sitting across the table from you. This is a MUST read for anyone who wants to live their life and make a difference."

-*Alice M. Richter*, Corporate Board Director, Retired KPMG Partner

"Bold Leadership requires a clear sense of self and continually striving to be and do better. For those wanting a bolder, more intentional and purpose-filled path, Nancy has written a mentor's guide to personal understanding and leadership. She speaks to you in the first person, using stories from work, family, friends, and school to pull you into the ideas. It's as if she's sitting across from you sharing and guiding. Reading her book is a very warm and encouraging place to be."

-*Chris LaVictoire Mahai*, Managaing Partner, Aveus LLC Author of ROAR: Strengthening business performance through speed, predictability, flexibility and leverage.

"Too often we see self-betterment as a radical alteration not only of behavior but of character, a matter of becoming, in other words, a new person rather than a better version of our real selves. With illustrations drawn from professional and family life, from sales trips and snowmobile adventures, GROUNDED demonstrates that true success depends on a lifelong process of self-discover, of seeking and analyzing candid feedback, optimizing your core strengths, and bringing out the best in others. As an executive, Nancy M. Dahl has provided the collaborative, intentional leadership needed to enact transformational change; her book GROUNDED will be an inspiration whether you're just starting out in a career or looking to sharpen your skills from a C-level office."

-*Nina Hale*, advertising executive and agency founder

"By sharing her own personal stories, Nancy shows us how important the human connection is to successful leadership. GROUNDED teaches us how to learn to live and lead your life with intention. The process builds confidence you can do it even when you are in doubt. The lessons provide insights that help you know what REALLY matters in your life, confident in your ability to make it up and correct on the fly and focused on celebrating your forward movement at every turn."

-*Martha Pomerantz*, Partner, Manager of Minneapolis Office, Evercore Wealth Management

"Grounded is a practical, no-nonsense approach to building the self-awareness essential to leadership excellence."

-*Mary Meehan*, CEO Co-founder, Panoramix Global

"Grounded was life-giving. It was exactly the book I needed today. This handbook for intentional living provides clarity that cuts through the chaos of the modern world.

Readers can't help but feel they have been gifted an opportunity to soar 10,000 feet above their lives and gain perspective on all that lies below.

Grounded encapsulates the wisdom and stories our generation so desparately needs and is searching for. This book could be considered the millennials' guidebook to a fulfilling and successful life.

Our generation will thrive if we manage to live life as intentionally, fiercely and gracefully as Nancy has."

-*Kelsie Schmit*, International MBA Graduate Student, IESE Business School, Barcelona, Spain

"Grounded - Leading your Life with Intention is a great read and lays out how to live the life you desire rather than simply accepting what is handed to you. Nancy taught me many of the principles of leading a life with intention during the years I was under her leadership and they have made a meaningful difference in my life."

-*David A Deal*, COO, Aspen Beverage Group

"Grounded captures Nancy's broad executive experiences in an accessible way to facilitate application for you and your own career/life phases. Nancy supports your thinking and development process by breaking the process into manageable components. The reader gains insight that makes it possible to reframe your perspective and direction. Enjoy! It's the beginning of an awesome journey called your life."

-*Grayce Belvedere-Young*, Founder & CEO, Lily Pad Consulting

"Grounded is inspiring, authentic and practical! Nancy Dahl shares her wisdom in a real way that will allow you to gain momentum not only for your career growth but also for your personal growth as well."

-*Amy Langer*, Co-Founder, SALO LLC

"Life lessons wrapped through storytelling is Nancy's gift for everyone--from young professionals who are wanting to advance their career to seasoned executives considering their next chapter. Grounded is filled with wisdom that brings new insight and inspires the reader to be intentional about what they want out of life. After all, the impact of our life's work is too important to leave to chance."

-*Jan Haeg*, Director of Field Talent Development, Lifetouch

"GROUNDED enables powerful conversations to address real world issues in our personal and professional lives. The work of understanding yourself has never been more essential. You need to be fully GROUNDED to lead both yourself and others, or risk getting in your own way and stopping the very progress you are trying to lead."

-*Lori Larson*, Learning Manager at a major financial services company

"Grounded provides a real-world perspective to leading your life starting with you. If you want to make the news in your life vs. just report it, GROUNDED is a must read."

-*Dan Mallin*, Managing Partner/Founder Equals 3, LLC, Corporate Board Director

"Soar with Nancy on her snowmobile as you learn the steps you need to take control of your destiny in her book GROUNDED. In the contemporary digital economy, we can no longer count on a steady ascent up the career ladder. Most of us at one time or another will plunge into the unknown. Through GROUNDED connect with Nancy's "raw courage and skill" as a guide to learn how to navigate to the next patch of solid ground.

-*Stefanie Ann Lenway*, Dean, Opus College of Business, University of St. Thomas, Minneapolis- St. Paul, Minnesota

"I am encouraged by the growing number of school districts implementing personalized learning in their respective communities to reach every student. GROUNDED takes a similar approach to working professionals in any field who wish to take their careers to the next level and beyond. We don't operate in a one size fits all world. Chapter by chapter, Nancy M. Dahl provides a turn-key approach to help the reader build his or her brand, professionally and personally."

-*Daniel Domenech*, Executive Director, American Association of School Administrators, Washington D.C.

"Lesson 11: If you are a 'guardian of gridlock', this book is not for you. If, on the other hand, you want to listen to your inner voice, think about 'you', and sort out your place in this big, big world of opportunity, read on. You'll thoroughly enjoy Nancy's thoughtful and thought-provoking approach in her book GROUNDED."

-*Jeff Prouty*, Chairman and Founder, The Prouty Project

"Nancy M. Dahl's energetic and optimistic book has ideas and advice that can serve us well throughout our personal and professional lives. Here are concepts that popped off the page for me: Mastery; Skill; Intentionality, curiosity, reflection, relationships; collaboration. You will hit the ground running after reading GROUNDED!"

-*Sarah Caruso*, President & CEO, Greater Twin Cities United Way

"Leading schools in the 21st century has never been as challenging as it is today, and navigating innovation and change in schools can be a lonely, difficult job. Nancy's straightforward approach to self-discovery, self-awareness, and self-actualization is exactly what educational leaders need to be successful and to inspire others. Learning how to manage emotions, learning the value of the debrief, and learning that sometimes we need to go slow to go fast...Nancy will be your leadership coach, helping you be the best leader - and the best person - you can be. I can't imagine how different my leadership journey would have been if I had never met Nancy. She truly walks the talk! GROUNDED is a must-read for all courageous educators ready to grow a culture of innovation in their school or district while inspiring others on their leadership journey and confronting the Guardians of No Progress!"

-*Eric Schneider*, Assistant Superintendent for Instruction at Minnetonka Public Schools

"Grounded is just that – a practical, no-nonsense guide to leadership."

-*David Hakensen*, Senior Public Relations Executive at a global communications firm

# CONTENTS

# FOREWORD

*I*n a world that seems to go faster, get noisier, and exist in a state of constant motion, finding your own peace in the chaos is hard. Only when you understand that the world isn't set up to optimize you can you begin your journey of discovery—to uncover what your "best" looks like.

It's a lifelong journey of discovery that some never take frankly because doing so is too difficult, they don't believe it will matter, or they think they can fool the process and find shortcuts. Still, others stop short of the true discovery that unleashes their power, passion, and purpose.

> *"We can do anything we want to if we stick to it long enough."*
>
> *—Helen Keller*

Your life is too important to leave it to chance. I wrote this book to encourage you to lead your life with intention, grounded in what matters to you. If you start with intention and the curiosity to understand yourself, you're able to find the best version of yourself because leadership is first a personal endeavor that starts from the inside out. You simply can't lead others unless you lead yourself first. Bottom line: life is the ultimate experience model. You don't come with an operating manual that tells you how to be your best. You just have to figure it out to find the things that work.

And the discovery is never done. You always have something else to learn. Dedicating yourself to the lifelong discipline of practice allows you to see what works. By committing to remain engaged in your journey, you can stay in tune with what grounds you at every turn. This understanding will allow you to master what is possible for you, and ultimately, others. The questions change as people move through their lives. In their twenties, people wonder where to begin. In their thirties, they wonder if they're headed in the right direction. In their forties, they may begin to wonder if this is all there is. And in their fifties and beyond, they wonder what should happen in the next chapter.

The power of understanding your personal foundation grounds you in what matters. It allows you to understand how you really work. Furthermore, it keeps you from being confused by the chaos in your world that can cause you to believe something else about you. Instead, your grounded perspective *and* your commitment to stay curious in your life make you unstoppable, even in rough waters. They make leading others possible. Without first knowing yourself, you have nothing to give.

Your life *will* have an impact. And you shouldn't leave it up to someone else to decide what that should be. Your life is too important. The choice is yours, unless you opt out—then someone else will decide.

That's why I wrote this book. Everyone thinks that he or she is in it alone. And everyone is, unless he or she reaches out to others to compare notes. It's only then that you can realize that you're more alike than different. You must be willing to share your own stories and be open to conversation to receive the same from others.

In fact, I wouldn't have written this book without the many conversations I've had with others. Ultimately, my friends and colleagues urged me to commit these conversations to a book to share the lessons with others. This book is the culmination of years of conversations over a glass of wine, during a walk, on a trip, or wherever I could find time to connect with others. The endless notes on scraps of paper and cocktail napkins and in the margins of articles were piling up in a folder until, one day, I couldn't ignore the work I'd done and the resounding support I had to write a book.

I love working in this zone, one focused on understanding my personal foundation so I can be intentional in my life. In fact, my personal mission statement is to bring relevance and high performance toward a future goal. Yet writing this book proved to be one of the hardest and most terrifying things I have ever done. If it weren't for the support of my friends, especially Tammie Lynn, this book would have remained a pile of notes in my folder to be considered someday.

Writing a book is something that many say they'll do because it's a sexy thing to talk about, but few actually make it happen. Because the work is real, it's hard, and it's not very sexy. Just as in your life journey, sometimes it takes others to believe in you before you do. I'm thankful for the support I had to bring this idea to reality and, most important, in a form that I can share with people I know and people I have yet to meet.

I dedicate this book to those individuals who wish to make their life journey intentional and those who wish to make the news in their life rather than just report it. And the work of grounding yourself first is essential if you wish to lead others and ultimately inspire others to be better than they dreamed possible.

This book requires you to do the work that grounds you in what matters most. It's about building a strong foundation that will guide you and your leadership regardless of your age or life experience. This book is really about the work.

This notion of being grounded isn't about age. It's a state of understanding more about you and what matters most to you and how finding your optimal state makes optimizing others possible. And finally, it's about making the world a better place, one person at a time, starting with you.

In the end, I hope the book impacts your life and inspires you to live your life to your full potential and to lead others so that 1 + 1 = 3. The questions raised are designed to "haunt" you—in a good way. They're simple questions to ask yourself, but they're hard to answer, and only you can do the work. So, like many things in life, you get to choose: If not now, then when?

I hope that the questions raised will play in your head like a song as a reminder that your life needs to be awesome—designed for you, by you, in a constant state of refinement. You're far too smart to be the only thing standing in your way. With focus and a commitment to practice, anything is possible. The important thing is that you start from wherever you are. The rest of your journey ahead is worth it, because it's for *you*.

Your best chapter is yet to come, and I look forward to hearing from you. You can share your feedback at www.nancymdahl.com or in person as I travel the world speaking to organizations that have started their journey to be their best. Comparing notes will help both of us be better. And isn't that the only true dimension of how you and I can impact this world in a way that matters?

# SECTION I: TAKING OWNERSHIP

**The Journey Begins . . .**

The notion of leading your life requires you to discover who you are so you're grounded and understand what really matters. And it isn't a one-and-done exercise, because things change. It's a lifelong journey to build discovery skills focused on you. Funny, how you spend 24/7 with yourself, but you're often the hardest to get to know. Doing so takes both intention and tenacity to master this mind-set.

> *"No person is free who is not a master of himself."*
>
> —*Epictetus*

Mastery means you intellectually understand and have command of your emotional makeup and your physical actions. Mastery means you can live in alignment and exercise your intention to optimize your life. What screws many people up is the picture they have of them in their head. But the picture isn't reality—it's your interpretation of reality. Ironically, the thing that often stops you from making significant progress in your life isn't somebody else's ideas, but your own self-limiting perceptions and beliefs. Letting go of the picture can be hard. You need to learn to trust your gut. The gut knows what the head hasn't figured out. I dedicate this section of this book to learning how to get out of your own way so you can be *awesome*. Being awesome won't happen by chance and can only happen with focus and willingness to change.

I'll share my process and why I continue to do what I do. I'll use examples and break the phases down into smaller parts to help you get started. This process may feel awkward at first, and potentially uncomfortable, but over time the behaviors become second nature. And you'll learn to be comfortable with the uncomfortable, because that's what is required to make true change.

# 1

# BEING A STUDENT OF YOU

*I*'ve heard it said that to truly master anything you have to spend ten thousand hours practicing your craft—a tall order for sure, and that's why many people fall short.

Here's the deal: skills are built through repetition, or practice. Think about something you learned. Whether it was riding a bike, mastering a school subject, excelling in a sport, or being an effective public speaker, all required practice. Sometimes you fell, or made a mistake. Welcome to the club. Other times you learned to push it further and go faster, showing yourself and others what is possible. Sometimes you win, and sometimes you learn.

This is how you develop the muscle to be intentional in your life every day. But learning to be intentional is unlike the skills you learned to ride a bike, where once you learned it, you were done. This muscle is built over a lifetime, because as the context of your life changes, you need to know how to unlearn, relearn, and learn again. Or in some cases, discover and learn it for the first time. Bottom line, you need to forever be a student of you in order to optimize both your quality and joy in life. Your focus needs to be on building the muscle and the process, not just the answers.

> *"And at the end of the day, your feet should be dirty, your hair messy, and your eyes sparkling."*
>
> —*Shanti*

3

How many times in your life have you run into a situation that didn't go well, leading you to think, "Well that's how I've done it before. Why didn't it work this time?" What likely happened is you had learned a skill previously, tried to apply the skill in a new situation, and it didn't perform the same. Your skill at the task was likely there, but your skill as a student of you wasn't. You weren't engaged in learning more—only in doing it just as you'd done before—so you weren't able to optimize your skill in the new situation. This, in turn, likely caused others to pick up the slack and you to wonder why you hadn't been more effective.

When others know more about you than you do, the advantage flips against you—people will use their knowledge of you to make choices for your life. I've seen it happen over and over again. It's your life, and you need to learn to control the aspects of life that are in your control. Helping people achieve this is a big part of my motivation for writing this book. The skill of being a student of you keeps you in the driver's seat of your own bus, which is the only seat you should ever occupy.

To clarify, when I say "control" your life, I don't mean you can control every detail; however, you can control the direction, which is an important distinction that helps you focus on the right things. If you've done your homework, and truly understand yourself, you're in a better position to optimize the moves that come at you and accelerate the pace of your decision-making.

Think about it.

Like most people, you have probably had a road trip that didn't go your way. But because you knew where you were going, you maneuvered around the road construction, figured out where the gas station was, fixed a flat tire, and still arrived to your destination. You didn't control every move, but you did control the direction. In some cases, those back roads showed you something extra that wasn't part of the original journey. That's true in life too. You just have to stay open to being the student so you don't get focused on your frustration of controlling every move and miss the key lessons that are there if you're willing to stay engaged and intentional in your life.

# BEING A STUDENT OF YOU

The commitment to studying yourself has always been important—not always understood, but always important. It was a difficult concept for me to embrace initially, and I know that's true of others as well. Why is this? Because being a student of oneself requires a curiosity about you that you may not be willing to commit to. Lack of curiosity seems to happen for three reasons:

- You get lazy because it's easier to do things the same way than to learn new things.

- A traumatic life event has "frozen" you in place.

- You simply don't believe that you can be intentional because life just happens to you.

For me, this notion of being intentional started in my hometown, a small community with only eight hundred people, many of whose families had lived there for generations. I had forty-two people in my graduation class and because everyone's family history was well known, a person's last name often became a life sentence, defining what others thought that person would or should do with his or her life—good or bad. I saw these prejudged life sentences lived out every day, and frankly I didn't like it. Why shouldn't I have some say in how and what I would do with my life? My journey began.

## Finding Your Own Path

Years later, I saw this same scenario lived out with my own sons in the Twin Cities, a much bigger city. My older son, Erik, was two feet when he was born and grew to be six eight. People had expectations of what he should do, what positions he should play in sports, and how he should live his life. When his younger brother, Jorgen, came along, he followed in Erik's shadow—literally and figuratively. They played the same sports in school with many of the same coaches. Jorgen fought to find his own place and not be pushed to play where Erik played. They were different people with different talents and gifts, not mirror images of each other just because they shared a last name.

I'm happy that one of the forty-two coaches my sons had over their school careers took the time to get to know them as individuals. Their lacrosse coach was a college student who grew up in our community and had played lacrosse. Neither of the boys knew him nor did I, but he clearly loved lacrosse, which was new to our area, and he wanted to help grow the sport by working with the youth program.

Making the practice schedule work wasn't always easy, but we found a way, because my boys really wanted to play. I could see the desire in their faces. They couldn't wait to get to the field to see their coach and the guys.

The coach arrived to every practice in his big black truck, always on time and always focused on the disciplines of practice. He pushed the boys, and when the players resisted, he responded with more running and drills. These extra drills weren't a favorite part of practice for the players, but they brought focus and built the physical capabilities of each player and the collective team. He had the same no-nonsense approach with the parents. He was there to build a winning team, one player at a time. He expected players and parents to make the same commitment.

The coach helped Erik understand that comparing his performance to guys half his size wasn't an apples-to-apples comparison. In fact, it didn't leverage the gifts that he had because he was trying to be like someone else. Although lacrosse often favors smaller, speedier players, the coach was able to show Erik how his larger size could be an advantage in his position, and that comparing his running times wasn't the right way to look at his ability to contribute to the team.

This insight made it possible for Erik to begin a journey of learning to practice and build the skills that were uniquely his own. The coach took extra steps to work with him during the season to help him practice his skills. Then the coach drafted Erik for a tournament weekend, which was considered quite an honor. He told my son that he likely wouldn't have a lot of playing time, but that Erik's size would be an advantage in his attack position and Erik's ability to block opposing players would be critical to the success of certain plays. This helped recalibrate Erik's expectations for his role on the team.

Just as the coach predicted, Erik didn't play much, but he did perform to the coach's expectations. Erik's performance mattered to the team, and he finally felt for the first time that his contributions were important. He realized that he could do things the other guys weren't designed to do. This coach led his team in a way that optimized and inspired greatness in each player. As a sophomore in college, this coach was already living what many leaders never understand: being a leader isn't about you; it's about how you inspire others to get results.

This awareness, which allowed my son to see his power for the first time, had a profound effect on his perspective and his life. He could now begin to play the game on his terms.

When my younger son came along, the coach's insight helped Jorgen gain a new perspective too. Jorgen learned getting feedback wasn't a sign of weakness but rather a sign of strength and a key to improve. The coach helped Jorgen see how conditioning could build his speed, agility, and confidence.

The coach's approach, the words he used, and his body language were entirely different with my two sons. The oldest one needed the coach to work right alongside him and provide real-time feedback. The coach knew that patient demonstration, practice, and words of encouragement were what Erik craved. The coach allowed my son to build momentum, mastery, and ultimately, the confidence in his own ability.

Jorgen required the opposite. The coach had to challenge him, get in his face, and hold him accountable to do the hard work. The coach's challenges frustrated and angered Jorgen, which in turn led to more running and more workouts. The coach didn't let my son's frustration wear him down. Instead, the coach continued with the same consistent approach. In time, my son's response changed. He learned a new way to play the game and approach life.

The understanding that both of my sons gained from the coach's insight was magical. To sum up their learning from the coach: my oldest son was meant to stop things, and my youngest son was meant to chase things.

Not everyone is lucky enough to have a coach who understands that the objective of leadership is to optimize each player. If you don't, you need to study yourself, discover your gifts, and make sure that you're optimizing them throughout your life.

*"Don't let the noise of other's opinions drown out your own inner voice."*

—*Steve Jobs*

### Anticipating Impact of Another Perspective

I remember the first time I had to deal with being judged differently because I'm female. I had always been able to compete in academics, sports, and outdoor activities, including hunting, fishing, snowmobiling, and skiing. I had never realized that women should have a different standard, that is, until a professor during my master's program asked the class to stand in line based on our survey score from highest to lowest. She then revealed the score was based on how we ranked against male and female traits. She explained that masculine behavior was at one end of the spectrum and more feminine behavior was at the other end. I stood in the number one position, demonstrating the most masculine traits. Mostly men and then a few women followed me in the line. A mix of men and women were in the middle and almost all females were at the other end. Even though I was in the number one position, I could clearly see that based on our order, that male traits were more valuable than female traits.

Outside of class and throughout my career, this attitude has been demonstrated again and again. Like the time when I was asked, right after earning my MBA, whether I was going to quit work and stay home and raise a family. Like when I was asked as an executive to help another buy a gift because "girls" are better at that. Like when I heard an executive say, "Women don't make hard choices; that's why we need to choose a man." Like when I heard a man ask my husband if I could be effective at my new leadership position in a woman-owned company, because the man was worried that two women wouldn't be able to work together.

Really, I was tempted to add a chapter called "You can't make this up." The number of real-life experiences that I've collected about how gender defines what someone thinks are a person's capabilities is mind blowing. For now, the stories sit in my folder to be pondered on a different day.

The lesson to be shared today is that no one deserves to be put in the same bucket based on gender or any other common trait. Others will always have opinions of what you should do. Ultimately, you get to choose.

Choosing may start by doing what you know, such as following in a parent's footsteps. You may feel most comfortable starting there, but I recommend moving from that space and exploring what else is out there. In the end, you may come back to what you know, but by following your own journey, you return with a broader perspective and many more possibilities.

I referred to this process earlier as "driving your own bus." The bus provides a powerful image for your own journey in life. You sit in the driver's seat, and the direction you choose is yours alone. When you are uncertain about the direction, my advice is to drive around the parking lot until the path becomes clear rather than parking the bus. Staying in drive makes finding the right path easier.

Furthermore, you'll never succeed with people who devalue you. When a person doesn't appreciate you, he or she doesn't deserve you. For me, I surround myself with people who truly value my intentioned direction and me. Thomas Friedman, the *New York Times* columnist and best-selling author, said it best, "If you are self-motivated, WOW, this world is tailored for you. The boundaries are gone. But if you're not self-motivated, this world will be a challenge because the walls, ceilings, and floors that protected people are disappearing . . . There will be fewer limits, but also fewer guarantees. Your specific contribution will define your specific benefits much more. Just showing up won't cut it."

The bus I've driven in my life's journey has taught me to be intentional in my path and direction. My strong intentions have allowed me to be ready to optimize the amazing opportunities that present themselves to me. I've worked at living an intentional life, and so it's become one of my strongest life skills. My dedication to practice has made living an intentional journey second nature for me. In the pages ahead, I'm excited to share with you some of the intentional practice strategies I've learned.

# 2

# TRYING ON "YOU"

*D*edicating yourself to the discipline of understanding *you* is a critically important life skill. It will take time, focus, and dedication. Studies show that to truly master a skill, it takes about ten thousand hours. The reality is that you build skills by actively being engaged and present in your life.

> *"The most difficult thing is the decision to act. The rest is merely tenacity."*
>
> *—Amelia Earhart*

Curiosity is the engine that makes it happen—the curiosity to ask great questions and explore perspectives from divergent sources. The more diverse your sources, the broader your base of understanding will be and the less likely you are to get pulled off center.

For me, getting feedback from diverse sources was critically important. I was able to cross-reference the feedback to build a more robust picture of myself. Working with a variety of sources to more fully understand who you really are can be both fun and daunting. But over time, the variety of feedback allows you to see your full power, so you can then begin to practice using the new perspectives and approaches gleaned from the feedback.

One of the more powerful experiences I have had was with a coaching circle of eight other people. The group was part of a life leadership retreat that I had enrolled in to help me get grounded in my current life so I could look ahead. All group members had received feedback from the other participants. Our assignment was to take time and think about the new information and then decide what we were going to do with it. We were then expected to share our plans with the others. I wasn't in love with this idea of sharing, because some of my thoughts were still unclear to me. I didn't know these eight people well, so I wondered how their feedback would provide any value to me and vice versa.

But I had no choice, of which I'm glad.

Our sharing is where I learned how our pieces came together. I remember the moment a woman shared how important my insight was to her ability to make a change. This group stayed together for six years after our three-day retreat—far longer than most groups. For part of that time, I felt like an outsider in the group, because I was the only one who was married with kids and in an executive role. But then I learned I could still provide—and receive—valuable feedback.

A lawyer from a health insurer who had a prescriptive approach to solving business problems was in the group. One day at our meeting, we helped her brainstorm three alternative paths to solutions. I role-played the three approaches with her that day. She looked at me and said, "I never thought about using these types of approaches in this way. You really push me to do more when you are here, Nancy. You up my game and help me connect the dots."

I was a little stunned, and in that moment, I learned of my power to "connect dots" and to bring clarity to others. Furthermore, I was reminded even though I'm good at connecting dots for others, I still need help connecting the dots for myself.

# TRYING ON "YOU"

## Choosing Assessment Tools

In the end, the longevity of our group connection and the assessment tools we used were a powerful combination in helping me connect my own dots. Many assessment tools available on the market today provide insight into who you are and describe how you appear to other people. Try some out and use whatever tools help you gain a perspective on you.

I have all my assessments back to my college days in a three-ring binder. It sounds crazy, but I've revisited the results many times to learn more, gain deeper insight, and help me identify key trends. Each review has allowed me to "try me on" and gain a new perspective that made it possible to develop an intentional plan to keep moving forward. Your job of discovery is never done, and revisiting these assessments gives you a foundation that continues to build as you add new perspectives, which is part of the lifelong journey.

I have my favorites: the Hogan Leadership Forecast Series, the Strong-Campbell Interest Inventory (now the Strong Interest Inventory and the Campbell Interest and Skill Survey), Form Q of the Myers-Briggs Type Indicator, the book *Standout* by Marcus Buckingham, and Gallup's StrengthsFinder,

The Hogan gives you an idea of what is important to you and provides insight about how you prioritize at different times of your life. In addition, it provides insight into who you are and how you show up to other people, including your how you show up in your worst day commonly referred to as your "dark side" and how you show up on your worst day. The picture that emerges becomes clear. This perspective helps you be proactive in managing yourself even on your darkest days. Essentially, it helps you be proactive so you don't get in your own way.

The Strong Interest Inventory and Form Q of the Myers-Briggs Type Indicator are powerful tools, but even better when you do both of them. Strong helps you identify what you like to do and the careers that match those interests, whereas the Myers-Briggs focuses on your personality type and how you think. Together they provide you a more robust picture of you that simply isn't possible to do with just one assessment tool.

Two final assessment tools are among the first to focus on finding your strengths versus working on your weaknesses. Marcus Buckingham's *StandOut: The Groundbreaking New Strengths Assessment from the Leader of the Strengths Revolution* book and website give you access to an online survey that helps you identify your strengths and provides a written report. The follow-up email reminders and videos help you practice being you. Gallup's StrengthsFinder also focuses on identifying and leveraging your strengths and bringing in people around you to fill in for your weaknesses.

## Using the Assessment Tools

Both of my boys took all of these assessments after they left high school, and they provided clarity on where my sons might want to begin their journey and the perspective needed to ask for feedback from others so they could learn more about themselves. Today, they reference the tools to figure out how to approach situations and to practice building their "muscle" to reach their full potential. One of my sons has taped a list of reminders to his mirror of what things he wants to practice.

For my oldest, the assessments brought clarity to the question: What should I do now? In particular, the StrengthsFinder highlighted three interest areas for him. He spent time interviewing people and then job shadowed someone for a week in each area. After each trip, he came home with new insights about what he liked and didn't like. He took the time to ask lots of questions and listen, and this careful process ultimately allowed him to choose a different college with confidence.

We had toured eight different schools, and the school he ultimately chose wasn't even on our initial radar. One of the people he interviewed suggested it. My husband and I were shocked when he wanted to visit this new college. As he reflects on it now, he knows the college he chose was the right place for him. The process, his curiosity, and willingness to listen to his intuition allowed him to find the right match.

For my younger son, the assessments allowed him to navigate a change in his declared major. Six weeks into his freshman year of college, he called me at the office. His tone and his insistence on needing to talk startled me. In fact, his call stopped me in my tracks. What could have gone wrong? I thought.

He told me he wanted to change his major. I expected to hear he didn't like his professors, the tests were too hard, or the people in his classes were weird. Much to my surprise, I heard something entirely different. He told me that he had followed through on my suggestions to interview people in the field and job shadow.

"Tell me more," I asked.

"Conservation officers work alone," he said. "I like working with people and competing in teams."

"What else?" I asked.

"They work every hunting and fishing opening, which means I will never be able to be part of our family traditions. Most of the conservation officers I met aren't married and I want to be married. And even after years of experience and advanced degrees, they don't make the kind of money that will allow me to live the life I envision for myself."

My son's insights about his major as a freshman pleased me. It allowed him to learn early that his initial choice wasn't right for him, so he went back to the results of his earlier assessments to choose another major. I had the same experience as a result of four internships I completed in college. The collective experiences, the curiosity, and the discipline to debrief from the internships allowed me to change my career focus even before I graduated.

Slowly building self-awareness allows you to "try you on" and ultimately "own it." If you do both of these, you're in a place to practice making "you" better. Ongoing, positive self-talk builds and changes your self-image. Your past doesn't equal your future. By broadening your perspective, you open new doors.

## Finding Your Sweet Spot

Knowledge builds awareness, which gives you potential, but you build mastery of being the best you through the discipline of practice. *Knowing without doing does nothing.* Practicing develops your ability to be intentional about operating in your sweet spot most of the time, allowing you the freedom to advocate for what optimizes you every day. Knowledge without the commitment to do is a waste of time and potential. Your potential!

> *"First say to yourself what you would be, and then do what you have to do."*
>
> —*Epictetus*

Because I like pictures, the Sweet Spot illustration below (figure 2.1) shows you a visual.

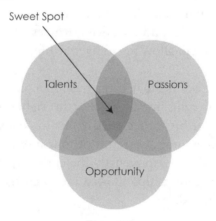

**Figure 2.1**

The assessments I discussed will help you get started. Each one will provide insights that confirm what you already knew or suspected and a few new things to chew on. Understanding your talents and gifts as well as your passions is critical. Then as you look at opportunities, you can overlay what is required and whether there is a match to what you love to do.

The best opportunities allow you to use most of your talents *and* work in areas in which you're passionate. Working in areas that utilize your talents but don't leverage your passions makes you feel empty even though you get feedback about how well you do your job. Working in areas that you're passionate about but that don't leverage your talents makes you excited that you're part of a mission, but frustrated that you aren't doing your best work. By understanding both your talents and your passions, you can be more aware of how to optimize you.

**Unpacking What You've Learned**

Remember, you develop a new dimension of insight and understanding that takes you forward in the doing or practicing. As you embark on your journey, take time to reflect on what you've learned from your practice. Unpacking what you've learned into three key dimensions as illustrated below in the Unpacking You diagram (figure 2.2) is important:

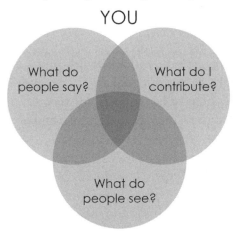

Figure 2.2

Unpacking gives you an opportunity to understand yourself from different perspectives and inputs. As you gather feedback and do your own reflection, first list the facts of what you contribute. Then list what people see. Lastly, list what people say. The goal is to discover how others describe you versus your own image of yourself. You want to have alignment.

Taking time to truly understand this perspective puts you in a better position to compare others' input with what matters to you. The human experience is made up of thinking, feeling, and doing. But remember that people can only see what you do. They don't know what you think or feel unless you share it with them. By taking the time to understand the answer to these three questions, you can understand your contribution from both an internal and external perspective, which makes it possible for you to intentionally manage yourself to optimize your behavior so that you can contribute at your highest level. Notice I didn't say *change* you. Instead, I focused on your ability to understand and *your intention on optimizing you*. Without this insight, you'll be responding to what others think you should be doing and not leading your life based on what matters to you.

Let me give you an example from my own discovery journey. I was talking with a coworker about how frustrated I was that a project was moving too slowly. I had just been promoted to a new job, which included my current job and two new areas of responsibility. My direct reports had grown from five to thirteen.

My coworker challenged me to look at my approach, suggesting that some people might be intimidated by it. He said, "Nancy, you're a quick thinker and seem to have all the answers, and maybe your team isn't processing it at the same rate. Slow down and be sure you're taking them with you."

I thought to myself, "Wow, slow down. What? It's already taking too long."

I told him that I always offered to help and that my door was always open. He said, "I know, but they don't want to disappoint you. Your team may not be open to discussing their thoughts before they have the answer or solution. You may not be as approachable as you think. You're very busy. Everyone knows that. And when you walk by, you're usually walking fast."

I responded, "Well you know I have a thirty-six-inch inseam, so I can take a lot less steps to get somewhere!" We laughed, but his point was a good one. *Perceptions are reality*. My approach was getting in the way of getting the work done.

As I unpacked the feedback, I could see that my contributions were valued—creating winning teams, focusing on results, and solving problems creatively. People said they wanted to be on my team because we would make a difference. They also felt that my leadership made them better and pushed them to do more than they thought they could. But what they saw led them to believe I was too busy to be approached and was a really quick study with whom they couldn't keep pace. As a result, they didn't want to stop me to ask questions.

I could also see the effect of not being replaced and doing multiple jobs with thirteen direct reports. It was affecting my ability to do my best work, and the rest of my life seemed to be falling apart. Even though the promotion was wonderful, it was important for me to be an advocate for what I needed to be successful. I negotiated a restructuring that reduced the number of direct reports, recalibrated the expectations, and reorganized the work to optimize the team's strengths. From this point forward, I learned to ask for what I needed, but also to be proactive about asking the right questions and establishing achievable expectations up front. Understanding that more isn't always better was a great lesson to learn.

Later that week I met with a mentor and discussed this situation with him. He confirmed my conclusions and added one more piece of feedback. He brought up the handwritten thank you note that I had sent him. He indicated that receiving a personal note was really nice. He knew this practice was important to me and told me he was happy I was continuing the practice even though my responsibilities were growing. He then shared that although it he appreciated the gesture, he could tell I was in a hurry when I wrote it, so it lost some of its "specialness." His feedback hit me like a ton of bricks.

Bottom line: people only see what you *do*; they don't see what you're thinking or feeling. What people didn't see was the amount of time I spent thinking about issues, considering alternatives, and collecting feedback—that I, in fact, didn't have the answers until I had done my homework. I'm a borderline extrovert-introvert on the Myers-Briggs assessment. I need time to process things internally and ponder the scenarios. Going forward, I needed to demonstrate my own process out loud so others could participate. I hadn't thought about doing things out loud before because I didn't want to waste others' time.

**Learning Out Loud**

I began including learning out loud into my process. Talking out loud felt odd at first. I had to fight the internal feeling of slowing things down. However, I saw the impact learning out loud had on my team's ability to incorporate feedback and move things along faster. It also made course correction less of an event because the lines of communication were established.

Learning out loud also made me more approachable and ultimately led to better solutions. It created a safe environment where the focus wasn't about the answer; it was about being curious, thinking solutions through together, and finalizing the action plan. This approach continues to serve me well. I understand how to do things out loud to expand my own understanding and bring others along, too.

As I noted before, the hardest person to really get to know is you. Think about it. You spend 24/7 with yourself. But you really can't see yourself except through your own lens. Seeking feedback is important to finding that composite view of the real you. But because you're programmed to gravitate to people like you, when you get their feedback, you don't truly see things as they are; you see them as you are. So seeking feedback from a more diverse group of people is also important. Doing so can be uncomfortable, but that's part of the process. When you practice your awareness and intention on getting a diverse view, you can build a broader understanding and a stronger foundation for personal growth.

# 3

# LEARNING TO DEBRIEF

*T*rying you on means you'll try on lots of different things. You'll learn to look at you from a variety of perspectives and overall experiences. It requires you to be engaged in figuring things out. You learn by doing. At first, being you may not be comfortable. The process of getting comfortable with the uncomfortable makes finding the real you possible.

Finding the real you takes time and sometimes multiple tryouts. Learning to slow down and hit replay didn't come easy for me. My excitement came in getting things done. I loved to check something off my to-do list and the feeling of working hard in finishing a project. Completing one thing always meant I was moving to the next big thing. I truly didn't understand the value of reflection, that debriefing with a team about the success/opportunities was a way to celebrate, to learn with a 20/20 rearview lens about how to make it better next time, and to bring closure before moving on.

These amazingly meaningful experiences all seemed to me at first a big waste of time. If you were there, you knew how it went. What else did you need? After all, the reviews I had experienced most of my life were test scores, report cards, or locker room comments from the coach after a game. It was always an event that looked at the answers and not the process. None of that helped me learn what I thought about an event, or what could help me get better if I looked at it with a bigger lens or from a different perspective. In my career, my performance reviews reinforced the idea that the boss, like the teacher or coach, set the course and graded the performance.

I finally understood early in my career and marriage the value of slowing down to replay and reflect on each experience. From the outside, my career appeared to be moving at a quick pace. I had a track record of nice promotions and new challenges. But inside, I could feel the tension. My reliance on one measure of progress was pulling me off balance. There was so much more to my life.

As I began to think about the collection of feedback over the years, I realized that I needed a broader lens. My accomplishments told only part of the story. The list of promotions and awards and my achievements in education and organizational leadership only represented my visible accomplishments. They were the outside story, but the inside story fueled me. How was I doing there?

## The Feedback Loop

I began asking for feedback. I started with people who were safe and knew me well, people I trusted to give an unbiased opinion, and people who wouldn't judge my asking as a weakness or lack of confidence, but rather as a sincere effort to be better. Life teaches you not to show your weaknesses, ask for help, or explore your thinking through your thoughts and feelings. People are taught to hide their weaknesses so they don't appear vulnerable. They learn to keep weakness undercover because the shelter offers protection. However, the opposite is true in real life when you're working to optimize you and others. Learning to look your weaknesses in the face and talk about them is a powerful way to connect with others.

My home economics teacher was one of my best and earliest experiences with having a mentor who worked to optimize me. She encouraged me to run for a state office with what was then the Future Homemakers of America (now the Family, Career, and Community Leaders of America). The idea had never crossed my mind, but she built my confidence to run for president. I ultimately worked hard on my campaign, but I didn't make it. I remember sitting in the convention center with tears in my eyes, but with a quiet resolve to learn more.

On the drive home, my teacher and I talked about the process, whether I should run again and, if I did, what I would change about my approach. I knew I would have to apply for a different position. The president job was a two-year commitment, and I would only have one year, because I would be a junior in high school. Her feedback and the way she asked questions made me able to embrace the actions I needed to take to change the outcome. She didn't ask me to look at what I did wrong; she asked questions like "What did you learn in the process?" and "If you were to do it again, what would you do differently?" The focus wasn't on her explaining all she knew, but rather on helping me discover the potential she saw in me.

I realized that my campaign experience had given me a broader perspective on the organization, which made me a better candidate. And reflecting on what I could do better, I decided I needed to practice my public speaking and my confidence. This was first time I had received feedback that caused me to reflect and debrief and empowered me to go to the next step.

The next year I ran again, and this time was victorious, winning the position of secretary for the state of Minnesota. My teacher's leadership has been a lifelong role model for me. She demonstrated through her actions and engagement what it means to recognize potential. She also was a leader who helped others discover and build their own potential.

The lessons learned from my home economics teacher have served me well in my career. For example, the process of learning to be clear about what I wanted and then having the courage, discipline, and openness to push myself has been the rocket fuel to stay the course, especially when I didn't get the job or the promotion. I also learned that taking time to recalibrate strengthens me even if it doesn't feel that way at the time and that the next leg of the journey will be better because I took time to take inventory and bring clarity to my overall vision. Remember, a life plan is about being directionally accurate, not about controlling every move.

I have continued asking for feedback throughout my career. But feedback is cheap, so you need to be careful to avoid the "hacks." Everyone has an opinion, but not all of them matter. You want to go where thoughtful consideration will be part of the process. I started small. I asked just one question at a time to get bite-sized pieces of coaching from various people throughout the year. The question focused on specifics versus a broad general question, such as "Do you have any feedback for me?" I'd ask something like "Did you feel my conclusion captured the main points of the presentation?" or "In this part of the presentation, there appeared to be some confusion—do you have any suggestions to make this clearer?"

I found some of the feedback odd. It didn't register as a reality I understood. Discounting the feedback would have been easy; however, the new perspective made me work at understanding what the person really meant more fully. When someone would give me feedback I doubted, I would test it out by approaching someone else at the meeting and getting his or her feedback on the same issue. Doing so helped me validate where I needed additional work and where the advice wasn't helpful.

I learned to practice asking questions about my work to a broad audience and writing down their feedback exactly as they said it so I could reflect on all the comments. I also learned to look past how feedback was delivered and instead focus my attention on understanding what they were saying. My determination to learn from whatever feedback I could get let me take charge of my learning, which I knew would be a key to taking charge of my life.

Later in my career, I learned the importance of advocating for my own feedback. Studies have shown that people who are different from the group receive less feedback on a routine basis. Not because some plot or scheme is in play, but because it's a side effect of how people are wired. (Remember, you gravitate toward things like you.) Building this skill will help you get the feedback that is essential to your own development, regardless of your environment.

I learned the value of this practice during a sales trip to a national retailer. I was traveling with our national sales manager whose practice was to visit a minimum of five stores once we arrived in the city before we would see the buyer. His objective was to see firsthand how our programs were doing.

At each store, we entered as customers first to observe. Then we found the people who stocked the shelves in our aisle, the staff at the customer service desk, and the manager of the area. Frequently, I would lose my manager in the store as he met with store employees and continued to ask questions. I observed how quickly he was building relationships. He asked questions about our programs, and he made them feel part of the team by showing them we were there to help. He made it clear their feedback mattered.

We would debrief about our store visits before we met with the buyer. My manager's approach had a profound effect on our ability to engage with the buyer. In some cases, we were aware of issues the buyer wasn't, and we could be proactive in offering a solution.

These trips allowed me to see the value of asking questions to gain insight. The trips were about understanding perspectives from the front line— about asking the same questions of many people and really listening to the answers. Our trip wasn't a test that would be scored and graded for just me. It would be evaluated based on the overall performance, which needed to include everyone to make it happen. This process made it possible for others to add value to the programs, too.

> *"Every person I work with knows something better than me. My job is to listen long enough to find it and use it."*
>
> —*Jack Nichols*

As I reflected on this trip, I began to wonder if this same approach would work to improve my overall performance and impact. I started doing trip summaries to keep track of my objectives, agenda, discussion highlights, and to-dos. Trip summaries allowed me to organize the immense amount of information from each trip into an actionable plan that would ensure that the to-do list was completed, but that I was also looking at the broader picture. The trip summaries provided an easy reminder before the next call so I could ensure that we had followed through on our commitments, could start where we left off, and offer insights to accelerate progress.

However, since the document was mine, it also gave me an opportunity to add feedback from my travel team and my personal comments about the trip. Did we accomplish the goals? How did I feel about my contributions? What did I learn and how will I incorporate that into my next visit? Because this debrief is in the field summary, it also gave me the context of the learning, which proved invaluable. I could see the patterns of my learning and the challenges that weren't apparent with just one single trip.

Over the years, I tweaked this field study process to help me clarify my thinking. One of the biggest changes I made was how I asked the questions. The process is about your future, so the questions need to keep you focused on the future and ways to perform better.

The question "What went wrong?" is easy but not forward-looking. Everyone has learned this skill in school when they reviewed their tests. Instead, ask "What would you do to achieve a better outcome, if you were to do it again?"

Feel the difference.

The first one shuts you down and closes your thinking. The second one gets you focused on solutions so that the next time you meet a similar situation, you can drive a different result versus feeling like "Oh, this didn't go so well last time." The first one puts you in reactive mode with hesitation and concern that history will repeat itself. The second one sets you up to move forward with confidence because you have thought about what to do next time. Then as you continue to think about ways to optimize your performance next time, it also gives your subconscious a positive record to play versus just a file of what went wrong.

At the top of my form lists my name, time period, position held/life stage, and a small area to describe the year in a narrative. This work provides a great place to trigger your memory about the context of the year, which is critically important to compare in later years. For example, it would record that you got married, had a baby, were in school, moved, changed jobs, sold your business, experienced an economic recession, mourned the death of a parent, retired, etc.—all important life events that affect you and how you show up. You need to have them recorded so you can remember as you review your form in the years ahead.

The rest of my form allows me to make notes about the details of the year as I debrief. I have boiled it down to four questions:

- What are my key accomplishments?

- What are my key learnings?

- What could I have optimized better, knowing what I know now?

- What do I need to continue working on as I move forward?

I answer the questions from a 360-degree view of my life, not just my vocation. Learning to look at your whole life, not just a part, will challenge you to integrate everything. The questions help me stay in the bigger picture of my life versus just looking at a component. It goes without saying that the majority of the notes will be on your vocation, because you spend most of your time there, but don't lose the opportunity to include notes or observations from your whole life.

For me, this process means taking a look at my well-being in five different dimensions. My career wellbeing, my social wellbeing, my financial wellbeing, my community wellbeing, and my physical wellbeing. People get focused in one dimension and starve another only to pay the consequences later. Taking time to really look at how you're doing against your expectations for your life is important.

I've learned this discipline of debriefing works in all parts of my life. I use these same questions to facilitate debriefing with my family, my staff, and my organizational work. But be clear, this isn't a formal white-board exercise. For my husband and me, it may be over a glass of wine. For my family, it may be over the dinner table or in a car. Many times the conversation can happen over a period of time. Each situation answers the same questions, but how you execute it will vary.

Bottom line: debriefing allows you to celebrate what you accomplish, acknowledge key learnings, bring everyone along because you're learning out loud, focus on improvements for the future, and identify what is needed.

I started this to practice being a better me. Over time, this process allowed me to earn the reputation as a leader who practices humility because I actively solicit constructive feedback. I demonstrate my respect for other perspectives because I don't believe that I have all the answers, but I do believe that together my team can figure it out. By showing your humility, embracing diversity, and working to understand perspectives, you build strength. I'm passionate about progress, not perfection in everything. In today's crazy marketplace, this process has also allowed me to be more agile in my thinking, quicker to recognize key areas that I need to understand better, and more effective in my decision-making to accelerate performance for my teams and me.

Over the years, I have found this process incredibly helpful as I would ponder the new year. I remember the first time I did this. I was enjoying time with my family over the holiday break. One morning as I sat in the quiet morning air with a warm cup of coffee, I began to think about the new year. The previous year had been a tough one with lots of moving parts and complexity. Bringing closure to the year was important so I could focus on moving forward. I needed a fresh perspective on the coming year, and so I began to debrief myself about the year.

I started with my field summary format and just started writing. The field summary was a nice process for emptying out my head all the things from the current year. By writing them down, I was able to organize them. I was also able to separate the issues and facts from the emotions, which is important. People aren't wired to have both an emotional and a rational discussion. The emotional will always win.

Because I had the benefit of looking at the year with 20/20 hindsight, I could focus more clearly. I could separate the issues. I could use my "wise mind," as Marsha Linehand coined in 1993, which balances the emotional mind—a person's inner knowledge and intuition—with the rational mind. This allowed me to be proactive. I could now see the emotional triggers, which made it possible to manage my emotions and focus on the issues without the unintended consequences of my emotions.

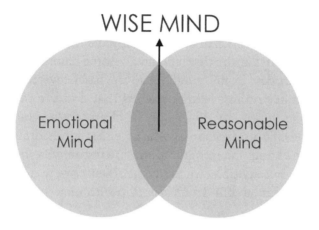

This process allowed me to accelerate my internal learning about me and see clearly things that I hadn't seen before. I realized, for example, that when I got emotionally charged about something, people saw my emotion, not my logic, and my point would get lost. And in those situations, if I couldn't control my emotions, I needed to walk away. It gave me the ability to truly consider my perspective, what other people involved saw and felt, as well as additional insights from outsiders that had no involvement. The combined input had a profound effect on my ability to learn.

The process gave me the benefit of slowing down and learning to replay an event or timeframe to truly examine the issues and results—celebrating what was accomplished, marking the key learnings, and pondering how to drive a better result. Celebrating also gave me closure to the year or event and allowed me to focus on the next chapter with a clean start.

Earlier in my life, I had experienced the same effect with the start and end of school. Think about it, you were able to unpack your locker at the end of each year and only bring back the things that you needed for the next year. Packing up your locker gave a sense of closure and a sense of beginning again with a fresh intentional start for the next leg of the journey.

On the home front, it has allowed me to see things that earlier in my career I might not have noticed. The wakeup call for me came one Saturday. I had been traveling a lot and was home only one day a week and on the weekends. I had scheduled my life this way. My husband and I had two boys at the time and an awesome nanny who came into our home each day. In my mind, I had the bases covered. However, I had put no value on just being there. As I sat down to catch up with my oldest son during my downtime, he clearly wasn't going to invest in the conversation. My happy-go-lucky oldest son had no interest in talking, even though he recognized my interest in what he was doing or thinking. I felt invisible. My frequent absences were starting to take a toll on my ability to build a relationship with him.

My husband and I waited to have our children. We shared the vision of building trusting, caring relationships with our kids. We knew our success at this would affect the ability of our kids and family to flourish, so I needed to make a different plan. My relationship with my son wasn't going to benefit from my efficiency. I needed to put more value on walking the crooked path versus the straight line. After all, if I lost some of my emails, I would manage. If I lost my children, I would never recover.

As I sat to talk with my husband, he too could see what was happening. But unlike me, he was home running his business and engaged with the kids. He had a good connection, but wanted a different one that included me. We talked about what was important and what needed to change. In the end, we took out our calendars and re-charted our course. We had children to build an awesome family, not to display as an artifact of the marriage.

We also talked about us. We were both focused on building successful careers, which was happening. Now that we had a plan to help us get our family on track, it was also important we do a better job of spending time together. When we had time, we spent it with the kids, which left little time for us. We felt guilty leaving them. We also put some dates on the calendar for us. We found ways to carve out half days to spend together while the kids were at daycare, or time for lunch on random days during the week.

> *"You will never be the person you can be if pressure, tension, and discipline are taken out of your life."*
>
> —*James G. Bilkey*

Over the years this discipline and focus has moved from scheduling a random lunch or taking a walk at the end of the day to planning short getaways and trips. Our first real vacation, just for us, happened fifteen years after marriage.

We went on a trip of the lifetime to the British Virgin Islands, sailing with a coworker friend and his wife, but it didn't stop there. During lunch one day before the trip, we decided it would be fun to invite two more couples so we could rent a larger boat. We all met for dinner before the trip to make sure it would work and we knew what to expect. Our friend told us to pack lightly: swimsuits, shorts, a sweatshirt, and maybe longer pants. That was it.

The anticipation of the trip and something new was so fun. The fact we would be in small quarters with another couple we didn't know was part of the magic, and so was the fact that my friend didn't get the boat booked until ten days before we left because he wanted the best deal.

Looking back, this trip could have been a disaster. What if we got on the boat and didn't like each other? What if all the boats were booked and we didn't have a place to stay? What if it wasn't a free and easy agenda where we could do whatever we wanted? What if—fill in the blank. Sure, a few things could have gone better, but mostly it was a great success, both of which we noted in our debriefing.

Debriefing is now part of how we do things, whether it's looking ahead or managing things on the fly. Our courage and commitment to take the time to debrief makes it possible to stay on the same page and have the life we dreamed of together. And for us, that is the crux of a successful marriage.

# 4

# GETTING PAST THE EMOTION

*E*veryone has had experiences packed with emotion. You know the ones, where long after the event, a mere mention still provokes strong reactions about the situation, the issues, and the people. Your emotional brain can disable your ability to think rationally, provoking anger and fear. Daniel Goleman, author of *Working with Emotional Intelligence* and an emotional intelligence pioneer, labeled this an "amygdala hijack." (The amygdala is the part of the emotional brain that controls the fight, flight, or freeze response.)

The good news is that extensive neuroscience research has discovered ways to develop new brain pathways. People can change their brains, but only if they deliberately force themselves to pay attention to what they're doing. The most powerful process for changing the brain is outlined in two books written by Doug Lennick, *Moral Intelligence* and *Financial Intelligence*. Both books are excellent and provide the background and the exercises to illustrate the process.

## The Magical 4 Rs

Over time, I have developed my own process for dealing with amygdala hijack, which incorporates elements from several resources. I also like the simplicity of Lennick's explanation for how to respond, which he describes in his books as the 4 R's: Recognition, Reflection, Reframing, and Responding.

The first R, Recognition, is a powerful tool, but only if you build the ability to make it second nature. Recognition essentially allows you to stop your life, hit replay, and see your patterns in thinking and emotion.

The second R is Reflection, which allows you to look at both the details and the bigger picture, including your "you facts"—your big picture and the realities of whatever situation you face. Reflection's primary purpose is to change the source of stimulation from the outside in to the inside out so you can focus your rational mind.

Based on your Recognition and Reflection results, you can move to the third R, which is Reframing. Reframing sets the stage for a better decision. I already talked about the importance of how you ask the question in the debrief process just as Doug Lennick outlines the reframing process in his book, *Moral Intelligence*. The debriefing question, "What could I have optimized better, knowing what I know now?" can help you recognize, reflect, and reframe the situation with this same discipline.

After unpacking the situation with the first three Rs—Recognition, Reflection, and Reframing—you'll have changed the highly charged emotion to a more calm and productive state. Doing so will allow you to improve how you're Responding, which is the fourth R. When in the Responding stage, remember not to rush things. Sometimes it's worth thinking through your response and then replaying the 4Rs again to see if there is anything else you haven't noticed or should consider that might help you.

**What the 4 Rs Can Do for You**

Building your 4 Rs skills is essential. When it becomes second nature, it will allow you to harvest the learnings from the past and access your current competencies to deal with the daily challenges of your life. This in turn allows you to build your competencies and prepares you to optimize your future without the emotional baggage of the past being dragged into the future.

## GETTING PAST THE EMOTION

Learning to be intentional in your use of the four Rs process will improve your ability to push through the emotional issues. Each time you practice the approach, you build your ability to make it part of your discipline, and it will show in your results.

# 5

# NAVIGATING OBSTACLES AND FORKS IN THE ROAD

*H*ave you ever bought a new phone . . . of course you have. I also have. Even when I know intellectually that it's time to change phones, emotionally doing so is a royal pain in the neck. I never enjoy the experience. Changing phones takes at least two hours—and each time I'm amazed at how such routine tasks take so long, especially because getting a new phone is repeated thousands of times for different people. How can this be possible?

Bottom line, changing phones drains my batteries. Regardless of your experience with this process, everyone struggles at first.

Why?

You have to be a student of your phone in order to know how to use it. You might start by using your current phone skills, but you find the buttons don't work the same, aren't in the same location or, in some cases, simply aren't there. In each case, you go from feeling like a master of your phone to an idiot. Even the basics are hard and the new features, although cool, aren't easy either. But you practice, ask for help from your friends, read the tips, and finally "voila!," you build the skills to optimize your new phone and all the features that matter to you. Through this process, you've navigated the obstacles and are ready to move forward.

As I mentioned in my foreword, this is a book about understanding yourself and your experiences and then applying what you learn so you can optimize your life. You don't come with an owner's manual on how to live and grow and develop.

I thought it might be helpful to share what I have learned along the way—truths that are fairly universal and can greatly affect how you work. (Or maybe it's my list of things I wish I had known from the beginning that no one told me!)

Think about this list as my life's cheat sheet, like the ones you used in college to help you study before taking a test or starting a class. But in this case this list helps you understand the context in which you're making life decisions so you can more easily navigate the obstacles and forks in the road.

- **People are wired to ensure survival.** Your brain is programmed to judge things and determine a fight or flight response. It is your default reaction. When a situation provokes this judgement, the brain sends an emotional trigger that makes it impossible for you to engage in both a rational discussion and an emotional one. This reaction sacrifices accuracy for speed every time. Learn to recognize it so you can be intentional in managing the situation vs. letting it manage you.

- **People aren't wired to multitask, regardless of what you think.** No amount of practice will optimize your ability to multitask, and switching between tasks can greatly reduce your performance. Your environments, which are becoming more intense, will control you unless you have a plan. Real-time access, anywhere, anytime, and the expectations of immediacy make it difficult to stay focused.

- **Everyone has only a few hours of peak productivity each day.** The ability to think clearly can vary widely over the course of the day. Know your peak productivity times and schedule accordingly. My most productive hours are seven a.m. to two p.m., and after that I have to do less impactful things.

- **Regular rest and hydration aren't optional.** In fact, many times, a lack of hydration has caused me to have a headache that can upend an entire day's plans.

- **Exercise or physical movements have a positive impact on how you think, encourage more discoveries, and feed self-confidence.**

- **People's ability to handle choice is limited to between three to seven choices at a time.** Keep the number of options you're considering to no more than five. Staying focused on a limited number of options allows you to optimize the results for you and others.

- **People gravitate to people and things like them and work to build from that base.** You don't see things as they are; you see them as *you* are.

- **An emotionally positive environment encourages learning by mitigating the big learning inhibitors: fears, ego defenses, complacency, and arrogance.**

- **Getting feedback strikes a tension between two human needs—the need to learn and grow and the need to be accepted just the way you are.**

- **People don't change until they're ready.**

- **In the absence of information, people always fill the gap with the negative version to finish the story.**

- **Unlike your brain and body, the subconscious mind never sleeps or rests.** The subconscious is working twenty-four hours a day and seven days a week. The subconscious has no ability to analyze any meaning, merit, or truth and has no logical or emotional reasoning capability whatsoever. The subconscious simply accepts and stores the data that it's provided and doesn't analyze things as positive or negative. The subconscious takes the data literally. The subconscious feeds the endless loop of conversation in your mind.

- **From the moment you're born, you have the innate drive to learn and understand the world around you.** Unfortunately, as you grow older, you lose touch with the internal sense of wonder and fascination and convince yourself that you have enough knowledge to understand the world around you. Losing your sense of wonder impacts your ability to lead others and yourself. When you combine this loss with your natural tendency to survive and judge things, innovation becomes difficult.

- **The essence of the human experience is building relationships.**

- **There are only 24 hours every day, which means you get 168 hours a week to live your life.** It's the same for everyone. When you subtract the time for sleeping and staying clean—sixty hours—and another eight for eating, you're left with a hundred hours a week. If you invest half of that—fifty hours—in working and commuting, you have fifty hours a week, two hundred hours a month, and twenty-four hundred hours a year of discretionary time. Learning to spend your time on what matters to you is important because it's *how* you spend your time that differentiates you and drives your impact.

These personal truths have become my owner's manual. They have helped me use my rational head to observe how life works so I can be more intentional in setting myself up to be my best. This list has helped me understand the context in which I operate and allowed me to understand more fully my natural tendencies. The ability to alter your course is directly related to your ability to understand facts, emotions, and feelings so you can do the right thing.

Your life's goal should never be to achieve perfection. There is always something to make better. Instead, your focus should be on seeing progress because getting to know yourself is a lifelong journey, which requires practice. And practice is messy.

# 6

# UNDERSTANDING YOUR FRAMEWORK

Your ability to move forward is directly related to your ability to practice persistent assessment that is authentic, transparent, and never punitive. The opportunity to celebrate your forward movement, expand your perspective, and refine your approach is part of your lifelong commitment to self-discovery.

The ability to seek feedback from others and yourself is critical. Revisiting old thinking and old errors and reviewing complex ideas from new angles allows you to see the progress you've made, how things have changed, and how outcomes were altered. It builds your ability to cultivate the wise mind I discussed in the chapter "Getting Past the Emotion" to develop a genuine humility, nurture your heart of gratitude, and build your courage for those times when it really counts.

The process allows you to begin to believe that what you learned is extremely worthwhile. It's about learning to celebrate the forward movement, not just the end goal. When you're finally in the space where what you feel in your heart actually makes sense in your head, you feel free to move along, but it takes a personal commitment to do something constructive with what has been learned and experienced. Otherwise, what was worthy of hearing, thinking, reading, and knowing never transforms into something worth doing or performing. It creates a knowing-doing gap, and the net effect is zero improvement with no conversion of potential to mastery.

But not all feedback is clear, transparent, and unfiltered. You need to take some time to think about the context of your experience so you can gain the insights.

To help you think through how it works, figure 6.1 illustrates the five major parts that you must consider to help debrief fully. It took me years to figure out the pieces and how each one affected the feedback and my interpretation. Now I go back to it frequently to review experiences in my work and personal life.

**DEBRIEFING FRAMEWORK**

| EXPERIENCE | EXPERIENCE | | |
|---|---|---|---|
| FILTERS | Courage, Risk, Conflict, Communication, and Curiosity | | |
| RESOURCES | **Health:** Activity, sleeping, eating & other habits that affect your health | **Resources to Leverage:** Property, finances, resources available from others | **Self-Governance:** "I know..." "I believe..." |
| BASE LAYER | "You" Facts: Values, Mission/Purpose, Talents, Passions, and Accelerators and Derailers | | |

**Figure 6.1**

The framework gave me a way to think about how to gather and think about the feedback. The framework also enabled consistency so I could practice and build my "muscle"and ability to process feedback as I learned to debrief and collect the key learnings that would assist me next time. It helped me accelerate my learning and be clearer faster so I can be nimbler and agile. I also use it to be proactive and anticipate issues, problems, and opportunities.

The illustration is built like a house. The base layer or foundation holds all the facts about you, which I refer to as you facts. These you facts are what your experiences are built on: your values, mission, and purpose; talents; passions; accelerators; and derailleurs. But the layers on top of that foundation can alter your feedback and your interpretation, which in turn, alters your future experience. Learning how you work is a process of trial and error. After experiencing a few bumps along the way, you can begin to size up how your internal process works.

# UNDERSTANDING YOUR FRAMEWORK

*"Repeat anything long enough and it will start to become you."*

—*Tom Hopkins*

Here I'll talk about how the framework works, big picture. Then I'll provide you a couple of examples to illustrate the application and power of its impact.

I've talked about the importance of knowing yourself. The more self-aware you are, the better prepared you are to do world-class work in all parts of your life. You gain knowledge of your YOU facts through analysis and evaluation of your experiences over your lifetime. Self-knowledge allows you to build your potential. Through doing, you build mastery of who you are and how you leverage yourself to optimize your life. Doing becomes the base layer or foundation on which your future is built. As life goes on, you'll continue to learn more about you and expand your true understanding of your foundation's capability.

Two key dimensions affect your experiences. The first is the resources you use—your health, resources, and self-governance. They affect how you engage. The second is your filters—courage, risk, conflict, communication, and curiosity—and how they affect your ability to see clearly and fully engage in the experience. They reflect how you process your experiences to learn more about you and how you work. When your filters are either too strong or underused, your conclusions will be faulty. For example, you may not push your curiosity enough to fully understand or you may not have pushed the experience enough to fully engage. Doing so will alter your future course from being your best.

Let me give you a couple of examples of how the model works so the individual parts make sense.

## Base Layer

The base layer contains all the things you know about you today as well as what you have yet to discover. The assessment tools I reviewed in chapter 2 can provide some initial input on defining your values, talents, and passions, and you can also gain knowledge and understanding of your "you facts" through the feedback from others and real-life experience. As you grow and change, some of these "you facts" will evolve with you.

You facts form your base layer. This is what you build your life on, so your ability to really know you is vitally important. Without this foundation, your house is built on the reality in your head, and it will shift because it isn't rooted in the actual reality of your life.

You'll go bump in the night as you try things on and figure it out. Everyone has had experiences where they're trying to do something, but the pieces aren't coming together. This is a great signal that there is more to know. Spending time in this space of discovery and truly understanding you is worth it. Find the missing pieces and move in the direction that fits you. Expect your list of discoveries to grow over time, both as brand new insights and as extra texture to what you already know. Both are invaluable to your ability to leverage your gifts in life.

## Resources Layer

The next layer of the illustration is the resources layer. It has three components: health, resources to leverage, and your self-governance or regulation. The condition of each of these components has an effect on your experience and your ultimate learning. Here, I'll talk about each one.

The health component is simply your ability to participate at full capacity. Can you play with your kids or are you out of shape and sit on the sidelines? Are you getting enough sleep to be productive at work?

The resources-to-leverage component includes both your personal property and financial resources. However, it also includes those resources that you can leverage from others to facilitate the experience. For example, if you work for a company, you may have access to a company vehicle or company jet, or you travel as part of your business. All of what is available to you is part of this component.

Last, the self-governance component refers to how you regulate your life. What are your rules of engagement? What do you believe about you? How does that belief show up in how you engage or what choices you make? Understanding how you show up to other people is critically important. If you're unaware of your own biases and the effect of your cultural norms on your actions, you can't be intentional about managing it. If you don't see them, even though everyone else does, they can have huge unintended consequences. Understanding your perspective requires both perseverance and intense focus so you can see the facts and the bias. Think about it as your own CSI-style investigation. Where you put your attention, you'll have growth. Spend the time to gain the perspective that keeps you in the driver's seat.

Let me provide you some examples from my own experiences.

When I was two, my mother discovered I had asthma and allergies. This condition became one of my health and self-governance you facts. Asthma affected my life experience because I couldn't go out for recess during certain times of the year, and I couldn't enjoy my love for horses because horse dander and hay exacerbated my asthma. I was forced to drop out of band because I didn't have the lung capacity to play the flute during those same times of years. I also couldn't sleep in a tent unless I was on a cot, and much to my father's chagrin, I had a legitimate excuse for why I couldn't mow the lawn. This knowledge, then, affected my self-governance—what I knew about me and what I believed I was capable of doing.

During my sophomore year in high school, I was part of the first volleyball team at my high school and had to unlearn and relearn my you fact and self-governance practices. I was really excited to be part of sports.

At that time, only basketball, track, and volleyball were offered for girls. I chose volleyball because there was no running like there was in the other two sports. However, during our practices, our coach announced that one of our conditioning exercises was going to be to run a mile. My heart sank. She asked everyone if there was anyone who felt they wouldn't be able to run a mile. I was the only one to raise my hand. She didn't hesitate and announced she would run with me. We ran together, side by side. Each day we went a little farther before I had to walk, but we always finished. Then finally, I could run the entire mile, which was the first time I hadn't let my erroneous belief about my asthma opt me out. I couldn't believe I had run the whole way! I had to unlearn and relearn so I could move forward.

Sometimes it takes someone to believe in you, and in those moments, you need to be open to accept the help. Demonstrate the curiosity and courage to explore learning again so you can unlearn and relearn a new capability. I learned to love running and took on the discipline of running daily for years. I learned to listen to my body and ultimately manage the asthma so I could make different choices. My experience with my volleyball coach had a profound effect on me and still does. My intention is to manage my health and still engage in the full experience. I now ask myself the question, "What if I didn't want that outcome and I wanted this one instead—what would I do?" To offer a more specific example, "If I don't like this month's sales forecast, what can I do to change the outcome?" Do you feel how these questions move you forward versus focusing on the barrier?

I'm certain that you know people who self-govern themselves out of situations or only participate in a portion due to what they know from their past. By doing so, they opt themselves out of fully engaging in their life experience and optimizing their full potential. Think about examples from your own life: people you know who have lost weight, learned a new hobby, or took time to make a new discovery and really see what was possible.

You need to be on the lookout and challenge yourself to be like my volleyball coach. Sometimes by believing in others before they believe in themselves, you can make it safe to ask questions, celebrate forward movement, and inspire them to unlearn and relearn a new approach. You need to make it possible for others to see what was there all along, but in a new light. Because you took the time to work side by side, you've unleashed more potential to make the world a better place. Isn't that a goal you can sign up to accomplish?

The resources you bring to an experience, including those you can leverage from others, can also have an effect on the results. I love the outdoors and everything that goes with that experience. I had always had the dream to go snowmobiling in the mountains. One day, my husband received an invitation to go snowmobiling near Jackson Hole, Wyoming, with a friend and a couple of his buddies. They invited me, too. I was elated.

When we arrived, we traveled up the mountain road to our hotel. The next morning, I was up early to enjoy my coffee in the mountain air. After breakfast we gathered our gear and went to pick up our snowmobiles. I had rented the biggest sled they had available, and my husband had opted for the next one down.

As I sized up the group of riders, I knew my husband and I were about the same level of rider. However, my husband's friend and his buddies were experienced riders and had much more experience on rugged terrain. I took it easy until I felt warmed up and followed others as we made our way out for the day. I was feeling good until I found myself stuck in a creek only thirty minutes into the trip. I had been following in the tracks of someone else, and as he crossed the mounds of snow, he hit the accelerator and the snow cornice fell into a creek below. I was surprised because I couldn't see the creek with all the snow. When the snow fell away, I had no time to react, so into the creek I went. Everyone had to stop and pull me out.

I was worried about what others might think: "Why do we have this guy's wife with us anyway?" "Is this what we have to look forward to for the rest of the day?" The voice in my head was having a heyday.

Luckily, it really wasn't a big deal—no broken parts and only lost time. And the guys were great.

But I was upset. I knew better. It served as a good reminder to "drive my own bus" versus follow in the tracks of someone else. I needed to run my own race. Playing someone else's game didn't optimize me.

We rode for two days in perfect conditions with awesome sunny blue skies. We spent little time on the trails and rode mostly in the fresh powder. I loved the views. Everything seemed bigger there. My snowmobile seemed to just float, and by shifting my weight, I could change direction. The only sounds were our machines until we stopped, and then the quietness and majesty of the surroundings filled our senses.

On the second day, I knew we would head into some more challenging territory, so I told my husband's buddy that if they wanted to head to the peaks, I could stay back. He insisted we stay together.

We took a break in one of the large bowls. The expansive mountains of snow and the blue sky were amazing sights, and the surroundings so quiet. As we sat and chatted, some of the group started up the steep sides, popping out on top and then coming back down. My husband's buddy encouraged us to join them. After some conversation, I decided to go. My husband stayed back.

The uphill climb began. What a rush! But what I couldn't see from the bottom was the steepness of the bank. As I approached the midpoint, I realized that I needed to stand up and press my shoulders toward the accelerator or risk not making it. There was no turning back, or I was certain to roll my sled. At that moment, I was so happy that I had rented this sled. From experience, I knew that horsepower would be my friend if I headed into challenging conditions. For those not into motor sports, horsepower is the "gearheads" version of courage. The more you have, the more risks you embrace, because you believe you can and know that you're supported. And when you get into difficult situations, believing in yourself is always your friend.

I popped out on top and turned to admire the view and high-five my husband's buddy. My adventure was simply awesome. Wow! Fun! Wow!

Then it hit me; now I had to go back down!

As we approached the edge, I couldn't see where I would land. I knew I had to accelerate before hitting the snow cornices or risk having it drop below me just like it had done in the creek the first day of our trip. Unlike the journey up, horsepower wasn't needed for this part of the trip. Instead, I needed raw courage and the skill to make it happen.

Off I went. One, two, three, Go! I dropped about three stories before hitting the snow and heading down the steep slope. It was a fast run down with no time to worry. Just pure adrenaline. What an experience! As I rounded the bottom of the bowl and headed back to greet my husband, I couldn't help but smile! I was happy that my husband's friend had pushed me. My husband could see that a younger version of me was back, and, yes, still a little crazy. He smiled, too.

I had forgotten how much I loved snowmobiling. Somehow, I had self-governed it from my reality. Now that I had kids, a big job, and a crazy life, I had decided my focus needed to be elsewhere. I had flipped my focus and frankly not in my favor. This experience provided a new perspective that would alter my future course. I came home from that trip with a commitment to pursue my passions in life, regardless of age. I felt challenged again to push the limits further to see what is possible, stay in my own track, and always bring the most horsepower.

My lesson reinforced my "you facts" and strengthened my understanding of my base layer. This experience helped me recommit to some "you facts" that had gone dormant—my passion for snowmobiling—and allowed me to see how the combination of my resources and my courage allowed me to fully engage in the experience. The snowmobile ride also gave me clarity about what is important in my self-governance—what keeps me inspired, challenged, and renewed. I knew this trip was the beginning of many more to come . . . and I knew why, too.

Think about the outcome of the experience. What would have happened if I had made different choices? If I had chosen less horsepower, I may have not made it to the top; a lack of curiosity and courage may have stopped me from exploring the trip or the ride that triggered this rediscovery. Without reflection on the key learnings, I may not have recalibrated my self-governance and found new clarity about what was important to keep me on my game.

Think about an example in your own life. Take the time to remember the event and your feelings from the experience. Then think about each piece in the debriefing framework diagram(Figure 6.1)found on page 48. How did each component perform and affect your experience? What were your key learnings and what adjustments or new discoveries did you make to add to your "you facts?" To get the most out of this exercise, be sure to journal your answers. Doing so lets you come back to the experience and continue to revisit your key learnings.

## Filter Layer

Now I turn my attention to the filter layer. The filter layer has five components: courage, conflict, risk, communication, and curiosity. For purposes of this discussion, I'll stay focused on examples of how they affect you individually. Later in the book, I'll explore the power of these filters on your leadership of others.

Each of the five can have a profound effect on your experiences, but they can sometimes be difficult to isolate individually. How each shows up can totally alter your overall experience and cause you to come to false conclusions. Learning to practice your critical thinking skills to build your self-awareness of your filters is vitally important.

Think about how these five filters had a profound effect on my snowmobile trip—the courage to accept the invitation, the ability to risk the hill climb, the skill to communicate and push through the conflict of going into the creek, and the curiosity to explore the powder versus follow the trails.

Let me illustrate with another example.

Going to Europe had been a dream of mine since high school. I saved money for six years to be able to go after college graduation. The year I graduated, jobs were tight; many of my friends weren't getting hired. I had a good offer, but the company wanted me to start in early June, which meant I would have to choose between the job and my trip to Europe.

Originally, I was going to be traveling with two other friends. We would join a tour group in New York before flying to London to start an eight-week tour of twenty-two countries. My friends both canceled in April and, besides that, my boyfriend and I decided to part ways. So there I sat.

What should I do? I remember calling home to share the scenario and to ask if I could move home and work for the family business when I returned from Europe. I knew I would be broke with no job, so knowing that I had somewhere to go and a way to earn money was important to me. I was fortunate to be able to have this choice. I still wondered if I would find another job. I worried about how long I might be stuck in my hometown before I could start my career.

After careful consideration, I called the employer back and explained the situation. I made it clear that this trip was important to me. I also thanked the employer for the opportunity and asked if I could be kept in mind for future opportunities. Before I left, I wrote a thank you and put it in the mail to reinforce my interest.

My courage to pursue my dream and curiosity to learn pushed me forward. I theorized that this opportunity to travel for eight weeks wouldn't come again. My assessment of the risk was minimized because I knew I could go home and work for the family business until I could find another job. I wasn't going to be homeless or starve. My communication with the employer clarified that this trip was a lifelong dream that I simply couldn't pass up and it should keep me in mind for the next round of hiring.

I went alone. I met the people in the tour group for the first time in New York before we flew to London. The trip was everything I had hoped for and more. I returned home eight weeks later with a great group of lifelong friends, a new view of the world, a letter waiting for me from the employer saying it was hiring again, and a date with my boyfriend the following day.

By pushing through all the filters, I was able to fully engage and experience something in my life that wouldn't have been possible if any one of them had been toned down or turned off.

This framework has allowed me to unpack my experiences into their components so I could identify the key learnings and understand how to optimize the next experience. As you'll see later, doing so has served me well in both personal and professional situations. Without the context of this framework, I easily forgot things, didn't fully examine the experience to identify a new discovery, or didn't connect the dots that would lead to a new insight. Now that I can reflect in a consistent manner, I can practice and build a skill that accelerates my learning, which makes me more agile and nimble as I work to gain mastery.

# 7

# LISTENING—*REALLY* LISTENING

*I*n today's fast-moving world, you're often under pressure to act now, rather than spending time to reason things through and think about the true facts. Not only can this lead you to the wrong conclusion, it can also cause you to misinterpret some of your feedback.

As you learned in the last chapter and chapter 2, practicing persistent feedback from you and others is essential to your development. Actions and decisions must be founded on reality. Likewise, when you accept or challenge other people's conclusions, you need to be confident that their reasoning, and yours, is firmly based on facts.

You face other obstacles to solid feedback. I discussed how the pressure of time provokes the emotional mind and how you can't have a rational and emotional conversation at the same time in the previous chapter, "Getting Past the Emotional." I also talked about how people gravitate to things like them and don't see things as they are, but as *they* are.

Sometimes feedback can help you avoid pain, but that's often because others don't want to hurt you and aren't giving you truthful feedback. But pain is part of the game, whether you're getting healthy, attending school, or growing a business. Working through pain is how you grow and mature. When people don't give you feedback based on reality or make you feel stupid for doing something hard or different, they aren't helping you at all.

In addition, some feedback can be based on cultural norms. Western culture tends to think largely in black or white. Things are either working or broken, and if they're broken, people try to fix them. But people aren't broken. Feedback needs to help people move forward, not just fix them. Everyone is at different stages of maturity, experience, and health. Understanding the context of the people receiving and giving feedback is important.

Culture can also cause people to confuse normal with healthy, so you get feedback based on the way it's supposed to be. Schools do it with children and corporations do it with employees. If someone isn't fitting into the normal patterns of a particular environment, it's assumed there must be something wrong with them. Society has little tolerance for divergent and alternative ways of thinking and living. Remember, people's natural tendency is to gravitate toward things like them and build from this base. Think about it, if someone is successful and unusual, they are eccentric. But if they're poor and unusual, they are crazy. In the end, people tend to pick on people who are different, label them as broken, and don't put in the effort to learn people's strengths, which they might benefit from.

Everyone's path is nuanced, and only the individual can find it. Don't hold yourself—or others—hostage to rules, platitudes, and expectations.

> *"Why fit in when you were born to stand out?"*
>
> —*Dr. Seuss*

The most important thing to remember about feedback is to really listen and hear what others are trying to say. Sometimes, you need to look past how someone delivered the message and focus instead on what he or she is trying to say to you. Don't turn advice or feedback into personal attack. The people giving you feedback are generally not bad people. If you make them your enemy, you'll feel more isolated than you need to be. Take the time to figure out what they meant, until your own mind is clear and confident. If you take the time to get a broad base of feedback and practice the discipline of internal reflection, your truth will emerge.

People also face their own internal bias. In the last chapter, I talked about how self-governance affects your experiences and the impact of what you believe and what you know. By understanding the context of your thinking process, you'll be better able to be intentional about recognizing your biases and working through them.

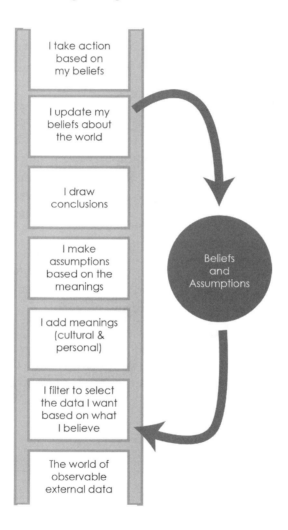

The Ladder of Inference above (figure 7.1), which was first put forward by organizational psychologist Chris Argyris, does a great job of illustrating this point.

The ladder illustrates the thinking process people go through, usually without realizing it, to get from a fact to a decision or action. Think of each step of the thinking process as a rung in the ladder. Starting at the bottom of the ladder, you have the reality and facts. From there you select the data that you want based on what you believe, then you add additional meanings based on your cultural norms and personal thoughts. You apply your assumptions and then draw conclusions based on the interpreted facts and your assumptions. Then you develop beliefs based on these conclusions and take actions that seem right based on what you believe.

This can create a vicious circle. Your beliefs have a big effect on how you select from reality and can lead you to ignore the true facts altogether. Soon you're literally jumping to conclusions—by missing facts and skipping steps in the reasoning process. Jumping to conclusions creates a version of self-talk that fools you into thinking that you're being logical and objective when you really aren't.

By using the Ladder of Inference, you can learn to get back to the facts and use your beliefs and experiences to drive a positive effect. Following this step-by-step reasoning can lead you to better results, and more importantly, expand your perspective and potential.

I have found it beneficial to analyze my reasoning by working back down the ladder after I think I'm done. The ladder helps trace your "my facts" and reality. Here are the key questions I use to work backwards down the ladder:

- Why have I chosen this course of action? Are there other actions I could have considered?

- What belief led to the action? Was it well founded?

- Why did I draw this conclusion? Is the conclusion sound?

- What am I assuming and why? Are my assumptions valid?

- What data have I chosen to use and why? Have I selected data rigorously?

- What are the real facts that I should be using? Should I consider other facts?

When you're analyzing, determine if you can skip rungs. Note your tendencies so you can learn to do that step with extra care in the future. You may find it helpful to use this technique with a coworker or friend to debrief after a meeting or project in which you're working. Debriefing with a friend allows you to see how each other thinks and identify each other's biases as you work through the questions. By practicing the skill of recognition, you'll be able to focus. Everything that happens to you is a result of what you're thinking, so by focusing your attention, you'll have the power to make change.

Be aware of the power of your conclusions to shape your future experiences. These conclusions will get filed in your self-governance guide as well as your subconscious. Taking extra care to ensure that your mind is clear is important. At each step you're building a stronger understanding of your foundation layer of you facts. Some facts will be updated or revised and others will be new discoveries.

> *"Unless someone like you cares a whole awful lot, nothing is going to get better. It's not."*
>
> *—Dr. Seuss*

This process of learning how you develop your conclusions is an important journey that requires courage and always leads to more insight, which increases your ability to leverage all of you.

# SECTION II: LEADING YOURSELF

**Keep Moving…**

So far you've spent time taking an insider's look at how you work—knowing what works for you and what doesn't, and what helps you accelerate and where you need to proceed with caution. Building your awareness makes it possible to act with intention in living your life. In the end, it sets you up to win and live your life to your full potential.

In this next section, I'll build on this understanding by focusing on how to build disciplines into your intentional leadership of your life so that winning is possible. The world isn't designed to optimize you. You need to learn how to become an advocate that allows you to beat the odds.

> *"The one who follows the crowd will go no further than the crowd. The one that walks alone is likely to find themselves in places no one has been before."*
>
> —*Albert Einstein*

As the lead float in your parade, you need to be prepared for the challenges that you'll face. Everyone looks at the world from his or her own perspective, so others may not get you and your plan. Learning to be confident that you know yourself is a fundamental ingredient in allowing your disciplines to develop and work, which I'll talk about in this next chapter.

# 8

# PUTTING THE PIECES TOGETHER

*I* love the quote from Brian Smith, the founder of UGG Boots. He said, "Even though I have founded and launched a very successful business, when I start the next one, I have to remember, you can't give birth to an adult." No matter how successful Smith had been, he had to restart every time and move through each phase again with his new venture. Every business has to go through the cycles and humans go through cycles, too. You have to set the right milestones and markers of progress so you can see them.

**Fear Is Inevitable; Panic Is an Option**

As you think about your life, the Smith quote is a great reminder that regardless of how successful you've been, you'll hit some of the same headwinds again in different situations. And each time you'll be challenged again, but you aren't alone in this experience.

Discovery is always fueled by curiosity. This skill will continue to develop as long as you practice a routine of debriefing to unpack the learnings. Then, as you make new discoveries or embrace unlearning and relearning, you need to make sure to celebrate each milestone as forward movement.

Now I turn my attention to explaining some of the critical you facts. The debriefing Framework illustrated on page 48, (Figure 6.1) has the five key components, which are values, mission, and purpose; talents; passions; accelerators; and derailleurs. They're the essential facts that make up your base/foundational layer. It's essential that you truly understand each component as it relates to you. The knowledge will allow you to stay focused when things get tough, allow you to operate out of your wise mind more often, and help you to be more nimble because you'll be grounded and understand what matters to you.

> *"You've always had the power, my dear. You just had to find it yourself."*
>
> —*Condensed quote from Glinda, The Good Witch in* **The Wizard of Oz**

Lots of tools can help you analyze your values, talents, and passions. I shared my favorites with you earlier in "Understanding Your Framework." Use what works for you and then use the combined input to finalize your list. Use the sweet spot illustration (figure 2.1) found on page 18 and the unpacking you illustration (figure 2.2) found on page 19 in chapter 2 to help you identify your sweet spot or to unpack the three dimensions of you (what you contribute and what people see and say) to see the common threads of the feedback you receive.

The work I want you to do next brings the power to help you understand you in context. I'll use the debrief exercises and the four key questions from chapter 3. But this time I direct you to step back and map your life. Yep, create a picture. Don't worry; it doesn't require being creative: just a piece of paper, a pencil, and time to reflect on your life.

Start by drawing a line across the bottom of a piece of paper. This will be the timeline of your life. Then draw a line across the left side of the paper. This will be the level of joy or high points in your life. Those two lines will likely be the only straight lines on your map!

Funny, when you look at someone else's life, you usually see a nice straight line. Maybe when you were just starting out, you thought yours would look like that too. But the fact of the matter is, everyone's life looks like the illustration below (figure 8.1), Putting the pieces together.:

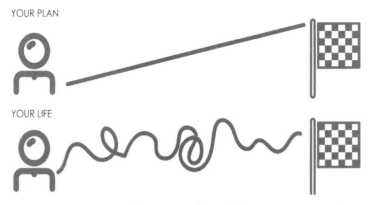

YOUR PLAN

YOUR LIFE

**figure number –8.1**

You can start the timeline anywhere you want in your life. The objective is to look at a span of time to see trends. Regardless of your age, I recommend starting with high school. Yep, I said high school. High school is generally the beginning of your story—the time you experience both highs and lows and many times some of your most meaningful and poignant experiences.

Your objective is to draw a line in proportion to the high and low from the start to the current day. Make a note about what the high points and low points were. Figure 8.2 below shows you my high points and figure 8.3 on the next page my low points.

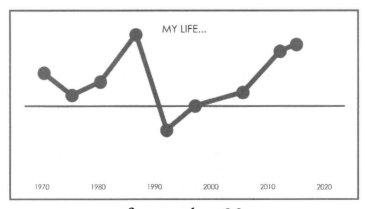

MY LIFE...

1970    1980    1990    2000    2010    2020

**figure number – 8.2**

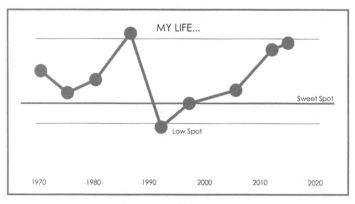

**figure number – 8.3**

The high points should mark times in your life when you felt you were working in your sweet spot and life was good, as in figure 8.2 on the previous page. By contrast, the low points are when everything was going in the wrong direction (refer to figure 8.3). As illustrated in figure 8.3 above, take time to reflect and recognize when you hit a transition point that made you head the other way. In other words, you hit a low and then one day it headed up. What happened and why? Using bullet points, write a description about your observations during the transition. Do this for each of your highs and lows. Then step back and look at it again. What patterns do you see?

I was amazed when I looked at my initial life map. For the first time, I could see with crystal clarity the patterns of behavior that emerged in the transitions. My line graphs and notes included my high school years, my college years, my early career years before kids, my early family years, and then my early executive years. The notes and patterns jumped off the page, and to think they had been there all along, but I couldn't see them. Now I could, making it possible to take this new understanding to optimize my future.

This exercise showed me in vivid color what caused me to derail and what helped accelerate my performance. It was a huge aha moment for me. The exercise allowed me to reframe each situation to understand what I could have done to optimize the situation, and in some cases, where doing so wasn't possible. Both were valuable lessons. I could see how my values, talents, and passions affected each situation. Over time, seeing the patterns and signs in future experiences will build confidence that you understand you.

One of the most amazing things about this exercise is that the patterns have been there all along. I have seen this happen every time someone takes the time to do the exercise. They just couldn't see them because the focus was in the moment of living their lives. As you move through life, the situations change and get more complex.

Taking the time to truly understand the dynamics of your history puts you in a better position to leverage your learnings to make your future brighter. Your past isn't your future. The past is only where you learned the lesson. Your future is where you get to apply the lesson.

The two biggest rewards for me in doing the life map were the crystal clarity and the ability to take the emotion away from situations, people, and in some cases, places. This new perspective allowed me to unpack my head and stop giving my energy to things that didn't matter. Instead, I could focus my attention on going forward and living my life to my potential. No more wasted time.

For me, the biggest epiphany, which was both a gift and a burden, was my ability to bring order to chaos and inspire people to unite around a strategic focus. It was a gift because I loved the work, and it showed in my results. However, it was also a curse. Other leaders, both internally and externally, sought my help to build their teams. Initially, I would be excited about the opportunity to take on the challenge and partner with their team. Then I learned the importance of spending time to understand the capability of the leader to lead through the change. I had experienced leaders who wanted me on their team because of my track record, but later they became intimidated because my leadership was improving the business, but not in a way that focused on them, so they would undermine me. In their minds, my work made them look less successful; they weren't capable of embracing the fact that I was there because they chose me to lead. In other cases, they weren't grounded in the reality of the business, so they set unrealistic expectations for the timeframe of change. These lessons became powerful and now help me make better choices.

You won't need to do your life map again. However, revisit the timeline as you think about mapping future events. The map brings new understanding and a plan of action to be intentional about driving a different outcome in the future.

The last piece you need to do is to uncover your true mission or purpose, and then put it into words. A lot has been written about this subject. For me, it's about discovering what you truly love to do and aligning it with what you do every single day. I didn't understand the power of this statement until I created mine at the age of forty.

I worked with a coach to help me take a full look at my life with a 360-degree view. One of my assignments was to create a personal mission statement. At first, I thought it would be easy. After all, that's what I do for businesses every day. This would be the same thing, right? Not. I worked at my personal mission statement nine times over a three-month period before I had one that stuck.

One of the things I noticed in my life map was what was present when I was working at my peak and what was not there at my lows. The descriptions of my transitions were critical to this discovery. This knowledge helped me frame my mission statement, but it wasn't until I was attending a small leadership group that the final word selections came together. The group gave me feedback that my biggest contribution to the group was my impact on their performance. They all performed better as a group when I was in attendance.

The final puzzle pieces came together. After three months of work and reflection, I had a mission statement. My mission statement: to promote relevance and high performance today for a future goal. The three key ingredients are relevance, high performance, and future. From that day forward, every time I drove home and replayed my day, I could see what ingredient was missing if it was a bad day or vice versa. This statement of eleven words has allowed me to be intentional about living this mission every day. Ten years ago, I revisited the exercise as I thought about my future. No alternatives rang true like this one—a sign that I had done the foundational work.

Some fifteen years later, as my husband and I were thinking about our lives, we did a similar exercise as we drove to see our boys at college. At first we generated ideas—what did we want to do with the rest of our lives? One idea per sticky note. No judgment. If it was unique to only one of us, our initials went in the corner. From that list we generated seven focus areas and set goals, dates, or general time frames. Then we moved to identify our top ten values. The conversation was meaningful as we talked about our ideas and why things were important to us. We challenged each other to give examples of how we lived our values so we could be certain we were walking our talk.

The exercise led us to create our own mission statement, which we had never done. Trying to do this as a couple intrigued us. My husband knew I had created a personal mission some fifteen years earlier, but we had never thought about this concept for us. I'm sure if I had asked him then, he would have rolled his eyes and dismissed it, but much to my surprise, he seemed to enjoy the process. The conversation drove us to see our mission, as we developed answers to the following questions: What are we most known for? Why do people want to hang with us? What feedback do we most often get from others?

In thirty minutes, I was able to get the words on paper. Unlike my personal mission statement, which took months, this one came much easier. Our mission statement as a couple is as follows: to create *memorable experiences* that build *lifelong relationships* and *storytelling for generations* to come. The words we chose mattered and are italicized. The magic of those ingredients defines our inside story as a couple. The impact was the same for us as it was for me as an individual. The clarity of the words on paper has allowed us to be intentional about living it every day.

This mission statement has strengthened our commitment to each other, improved our alignment, and delivered more joy into our life—another awesome gift from learning to lead our lives.

# 9

# UNDERSTANDING WHAT DERAILS YOU

*I*n the previous chapter, I talked about identifying what derails you—those things that cause you to go off course and not optimize your best work. This is as important as knowing your strengths, so in this chapter you'll explore what derails you and how to deal with your *derailleurs*.

I understand that this can be like going to the dentist, getting your annual physical, balancing your checkbook, or talking to someone about your finances. I get it. But it's a critical step in self-discovery and essential for you to understand. It has been a vital link for me. Without it, you can't build self-awareness and learn how to optimize yourself. So you can't skip it.

Instead, I spend time to desensitize your reaction to the emotion that comes when you think about these events and instead look objectively at the facts of the case. Think about this exercise as an opportunity to create your own episode of the popular TV series, *CSI*. You get to pick the cast—and the plot.

Your end game is to convert your emotional reaction to a rational understanding so that next time, you can take the same facts, intentionally have a new experience, and build your skill and courage to improve. Practicing this approach will build positive momentum for you and build the belief that even when you don't know the answer, you can figure it out every time!

Let me give you an example using my mission statement. Remember the ingredients? Relevance, high performance, and future goal. When these three things aren't in place, I derail and/or don't optimize me. Guess when those things happened? In periods of transition.

To identify my derailleurs, I used my life map and reviewed the trend lines and the details of my high and low points. The first time I did this exercise I divided my thinking into high school, college, and professional career. I had three columns. The first was simply the time period with dates, the second a short description of the high or low point, and a final column that described when each high and low started and ended. All the descriptions were specific but were listed in bullet points so it was easy to read and review. The same trend lines appeared in each section of my life, especially during transitions. Aha!

But guess what, transitions are a reality of life. Yikes! "Guess this is just the way I'm going to have to live my life." Not so fast! Remember what living with intention is all about: same facts, new experience, on purpose. Understanding the facts of your life is a critical first step to understanding where you are so that you can be intentional about creating an experience . . . on purpose. You leave nothing to chance. Life isn't what happens to you. Life is what you do with what happens.

By digging deeper, I clearly saw that everything in life has an ending. Think about it. Your food has expiration dates. You attend school for a set number of years. Sports seasons have a declared beginning and ending. You know that you'll die one day. But for so many life experiences, the ending isn't posted when you sign up or begin a new experience, so you can't plan for a transition. So these endings sometimes take you by surprise or leave you indignant when they arrive unceremoniously. That's why people often feel the sense of loss more deeply and personally.

You can't change the fact that you have transitions, but you can get better at anticipating them. I've found that anticipating transitions gives me the opportunity to leverage my best—bringing relevance and high performance to a future goal—all key ingredients for me and for those around me. In fact, I love the opportunity to be a student of the situation and figure things out.

I put my focus on learning to recognize the signs of transition before they happen. I also became more intentional at the start about declaring why I was doing something, identifying my key markers of success, and figuring out under what conditions I would be done. In addition, I spent some time anticipating the range of situations/issues that I would likely experience in advance. I was proactive and able to stay focused on the rational side of things. This put me in a position to compare my prework with the actual reality I experienced, and then course correct and add new information as needed.

This discipline also drove a deeper understanding of some of the "ingredients" that were in those low points. Ingredients include those things you would use to describe the situation, the people, the environment, your mood/outlook and issues in your life. In some cases, the ingredients were toxic, and in all cases they were negative factors in my ability to optimize both the situation and the results. Among the ingredients I identified as bad for me: highly charged political environments, environments bent on keeping things the same, and people who aren't confident enough to challenge and engage, but are quick to take credit or point blame. Building this clarity put me in a position to recognize the ingredients faster and in most cases take a different course of action or avoid it entirely.

In the end, I increased my chances of staying ahead of the curve to optimize the results and me. In some cases, it meant exiting the situation. Recognizing pivot points—times when things can turn bad or good—and having a broad viewpoint of the situation is critical so you can manage your plan and adjust, if necessary, along the way. Embracing this practice is important. You probably all have seen situations where people get terrified by the thought of bailing and stay in situations—marriages, relationships, jobs—because they feel they're stuck. It's your life—you always have a choice. But that doesn't mean they're all easy.

For me, my pivot points were related to either my opportunity to advance in the organization or in my confidence about whether the organization was headed in a solid, long-term direction. Each situation was intense, because it was about my future. In some cases, I had to unlearn some of my beliefs about my organization in order to move forward. Early on, it challenged me to examine whether I was living a lie, because I was so passionate about what I was doing. However, my conviction to optimize me coupled with my confidence that I could figure it out fueled my ability to develop a plan.

Sometimes you run into a situation that, regardless of your efforts, isn't a good place for you to be. You get to decide when your relationship with that situation is over. The commitment to stay disciplined allows you to see with clarity what is happening versus building a reality that exists only in your mind. The quicker you recognize the signs, the sooner you can turn your attention to moving in a different direction to find the next adventure that optimizes you on your life's journey.

# 10

# LEARNING TO NURTURE YOURSELF

*I* love both classic movies and children's books. As I spend time now as an adult watching and reading, I always discover something new. Maybe because I now have a different view, or maybe I just never saw it as a child, but each time there are great life lessons.

One of those movies is The Wizard of Oz. I love the movie. My husband hates it. He was terrified as a child of the flying monkeys and still won't watch it. I love the scenery, the costumes, the pageantry, but most of all, the entire overall message.

Remember Glinda the Good Witch from the Wizard of Oz??

She had great advice for Dorothy that fits your quest for living with intention. Dorothy was talking about going home and described it as a place. Glinda's advice to Dorothy was, "Home is a place we all must find, child. It's not just a place where you eat or sleep. Home is knowing. Knowing your mind, knowing your heart, knowing your courage. If we know ourselves, we're always home, anywhere."

Isn't that true?

As I have grown in knowing my mind, heart, and courage, I know I am less dependent on a place to find comfort. Don't get me wrong; I still love visiting some of my old haunts. The smell of certain places, the feeling of an old chair, the sound of a creaky staircase or old wood floors—the connections of once familiar places are all still magical. But as they too change, you need to establish that comfort within you so you can build your resiliency and agility for your journey anywhere.

## High and Low Points

Just as you looked at your high and low point work for what derailed you, this time look for things that you need to stay in the zone—the things that helped accelerate your abilities. As soon as you identify your accelerators, you'll take some time to look again at your "you facts" to better understand what you need to ensure that you're nurturing you. When you understand both your high and low points at a deep level, it enables you to stay focused on your purpose, keep your will strong, and remain unshakable in your determination to live your life with intention.

Now to start, go back to your high/low point exercise. This time review your notes about the high points. Look at the detail in your bullet points. What things brought you the most joy and sense of accomplishment? Write them down. Are they similar over time? As you read the comments, do they bring back that feeling of pride you had back then? What is the trend or commonality between the events?

I discovered trends and common elements in my notes. My suspicion is that you will too. Make a list of high points and then summarize them. Limit the list to the top ten. You'll notice two things. First, some of them are the opposite of what derails you, and second, they're the critical ingredients of your mission statement. The additional items in your list are likely to describe the environment, the kind of people, or the kind of leader that optimizes you. As you find clarity and add these characteristics to your "you fact" notes, you should feel like the pieces of your puzzle are starting to fit together.

Spending time on this list to ensure that you really understand it at a deep level is important. You'll develop critical insights from learning to recognize the evidence that shows where you're headed. Understanding both your derailleurs and your accelerators in vivid detail, without emotion, is vitally important. In time, learning to recognize either will become second nature, which puts you in the best place to be your own advocate and make good choices. Think about them as street signs that help you navigate the next leg of the journey with skill.

### Centers of Confidence

As you review your list of high points, I ask you to explore another perspective. This time, ask what you need to stay focused and strong willed and maintain your invincible determination. Look for those things that helped you push through, reinforced you were on the right track, or were the places you went to seek support. The answers will become your centers of confidence, which together will be the control center that fuels your ability to move forward.

Identifying and understanding your centers of confidence is important work. They articulate the core care and feeding activities you need to stay healthy and in a position to do your best work. By building a strong sense of what you need to be your best, you can be intentional in seeking this kind of feedback to help you stay focused.

Let me give you a personal example.

By looking at my timeline, I saw the key components that gave me confidence. When they were present in a situation, I felt confident. When they were absent, I lost my balance and my focus. This process allowed me to identify my five centers of confidence. They are as follows:

- My physical well-being

- Time to just be vs. do

- Time to being versus doing

- Verbal feedback/discussion

- An environment that aligns with my personal mission

In each case, I could find times where I hadn't stayed focused on that discipline, and it had a direct effect on my confidence.

They all take focus, but for me three took special attention to avoid relapsing. First, my physical well-being is a center of confidence, but sometimes I wouldn't take the time to stay in shape or eat right because I needed to stay late at the office or thought I didn't have time. Everything else came first. If you've experienced this, too, you know that, in time, it catches up with you, and eventually you don't feel your best and lose confidence.

The second area that sometimes fell by the wayside was making time to being versus doing. As life moves along, you can easily get busy with doing life and lose what is important to you. You lose sight of what you're passionate about and what brings you the most joy. You forget that sometimes it should be just be about you. I shared earlier the story of snowmobiling in the mountains. I had forgotten the fun and joy it brought to me. I needed to do it more. Take a look at your passions and ask the question, "When was the last time you spent time doing one of them just because?

As I practiced taking time to being versus doing, I also learned some other things. Initially, I thought my being time was just one big bucket. Later, I realized that I needed to refine my definition to truly capture what nourished me. I needed to focus on four key areas:

- Time alone

- Time with my husband

- Time with the family

- Time with friends

I struggled with this center of confidence—being versus doing—the most in the beginning.

Staying diligent in my commitment to practice all four areas was difficult. My tendency to serve others before me caused some conflict. The biggest one was likely with my husband. Initially, he saw my solo retreats to the cabin as a sign that he had done something wrong. As I Mentioned earlier, I am a borderline extrovert/introvert on the Myers-Briggs Scale, and he is a high E, so spending time with people energized him, whereas I needed a balance of alone time and people time. We had lots of conversation before he grew to understand and appreciate the importance of my time away.

Learning to separate friends and family proved challenging too. When our kids were young, this commitment to keep a larger focus took both of us to keep all the wheels on the wagon. To save money and reduce the public conflict of noisy kids, we would often host events at home. When the kids got older, I moved to scheduling time with friends during the workweek, either as a partial day off or just for lunch. Then, after many years, I was able to schedule extended periods of time with friends.

Intentional planning is what's needed to get the dates on the calendar to make this entire center of confidence happen. I think that's the nature of it. I'm still not where I want to be, but I'm going to celebrate my forward movement as I continue to stay focused. I now know the importance of nurturing this center of confidence to doing my best work.

The final center of confidence that was challenging for me was feedback and discussion. That may be surprising to you, but I've found I really need to practice seeking feedback from a diverse group of people versus relying on just a few of my inner circle. A broad and diverse base of feedback is my center of confidence. Earlier I talked about the role performance reviews, test scores, and teacher/boss/coach feedback had on me. I learned that pursuing a broader base of feedback was key, which was especially true as I was promoted to jobs of increasing responsibility. The broader the base of feedback, the less vulnerable I was to an attack on my confidence from one source. Developing and maintaining a 360-degree view is difficult, but it's worth the effort.

This broad perspective keeps you grounded in your reality, because it gives you a more expansive view. How many times have you been part of a conversation where two people were in the same meeting but took away entirely different perspectives? Remember, your hard wiring works against you. You're wired to focus on survival and to seek people and things like you—not diverse points of view. Without diverse perspectives, each person hears what he or she wants to hear and draws conclusions based on his or her belief systems. I've learned to use the debriefing practice as a discipline and to seek feedback from diverse perspectives to ensure I get the whole picture, both context and nuances. Without this broader perspective, I would fill in my information gaps with what I thought I knew versus taking the time to really know the situation from various viewpoints.

## Harnessing the Power of Your Subconscious

Regardless of what your centers of confidence look like, everyone shares one very powerful influencer—a subconscious. In chapter 5, I noted that the subconscious feeds an endless loop of conversation in your mind twenty-four hours a day, seven days a week. The subconscious has no ability to analyze any meaning, merit, or truth and accepts everything it's fed at face value.

Think about it as a direct feed of exactly what you say, almost like a toddler would repeat what a parent says or does. If you say, "I'm fat," "I'm not good with . . . ," "I'm clumsy," "I'm not a good public speaker," those messages play back to you over and over. If, on the other hand, you tell "yourself "I'm awesome," "I'm happy with myself," "I learned how to do something differently, and next time I will do [this] to make it better," then you'll hear those messages played by the voices in your head over and over again.

# LEARNING TO NURTURE YOURSELF

The subconscious is a powerful tool. You can't expect to live a positive life if you're around negative people and events and only talk about what is wrong with things. The same is true about your subconscious. You want the record playing in your head to be focused on optimizing you. You need to seek out positive experiences and focus your attention on positive messages to make sure that's what your subconscious is hearing and playing back to you. When you're in a situation where all you can see are negative messages, reframe the issue to focus on optimizing the result next time, not wallowing in all the things that went wrong.

I learned the benefit of reframing the message when I found myself in a very negative environment: a leader who was a bully, a culture that loved to seek out the weakest and eliminate them, and people who loved to report the issues but never offered to help solve the problem. I learned to take time to reframe the day into a forward-looking approach that optimized the situation. Reframing allowed me to stay focused on forward movement forward without the drag of listening to a negative message twenty-four hours, seven days a week. Reframing had a profound impact on my health and ability to stay focused on what mattered to me.

I also incorporated a new discipline in both my morning and evening routine.

In the morning, I think about my sweet spot and the work that optimizes me. Then I say out loud words of affirmation that reinforce that I can add value. Sometimes, it's simple. "I am excited about X and know I will do great work today." Other times, I recite a list of things that I know I'll do that day. Verbalizing it makes a difference. Try it. The practice may feel weird at first, but then you'll love the impact it has on you. For me, I started doing this every time I crossed over a certain bridge on my way to work. I had to say out loud words of affirmation ten times as I crossed the bridge, which was a trigger point each morning. The words served as a "breakfast" for my mind that powered up and enabled me to do great work every day.

In the evening, I think through the day and frame a question that needs to be answered in the coming days, weeks, or months, such as "How can

I bring renewed focus to growing our sales?" Then, I look at the probable outcome if there is no intervention (stagnant sales, for example). Finally, I ask myself, "What should I do if I don't want that outcome?" The questions give my subconscious something to do while I sleep. I know it sounds funny, but it works. The process of reviewing the facts is like pulling out all the files on the table so I can do the work. The forward-looking question poses it in terms that promote action. This discipline has been extremely helpful when I feel stuck or overwhelmed. This intentional routine of asking questions and focusing the effort helps me move forward.

### Practicing Your Centers of Confidence

Building discipline to practice in each of your centers of confidence is vital to your health and well-being. The practice requires you to be committed even when others question you. Remember, this is about you, not them. You see others not as they are but as you are—and vice versa, so it's highly likely that other people won't understand what you need to be healthy so you need to advocate for what matters. Don't waste time trying to convert them. What matters is that you have clarity about your centers of confidence so you can be your own advocate to make it happen.

When you get good at your discipline to practice being your own advocate, others will question whether you're too good to be true. I saw this with a football friend of my oldest son. Over his college football career, he achieved tremendous success both on and off the field. He was called a "once-in-a-generation student athlete." When the NFL scouts came to check him out, they took a contrarian angle. They didn't believe he could be as wonderful as advertised. His dedicated work ethic and extra effort kept him healthy, resilient, and agile to optimize his potential at every turn. Most teams passed on him, but one took a chance. He received an invitation to the team's NFL camp for a few thousand dollars and was offered the chance to try out. During the preseason, he was declared the most underrated player in the league. In the end, he earned a spot on the team and not only plays in the NFL, but he also is recognized as a vital leader for the team.

The power of his discipline to practice and advocate for what he needed to be his best showed. He is a great example of living your life with intention. By being grounded in knowing who he was and what mattered to him, he was able to focus on creating a different experience than others thought possible. No one said it will be easy, but the effort is worthwhile because you're doing it for you—your effort, your life, your impact, your accountability.

# 11

# INTEGRATING WHAT MATTERS IN YOUR LIFE

*I*n this on-demand economy where nothing ever shuts down or closes and you have endless choice, you can easily feel overwhelmed. In fact, this kind of environment promotes a perpetual "busy" that isn't designed to optimize you. That's why the remedy is to focus on being intentional in setting your expectations and developing your disciplines to manage your time, define your boundaries, and ultimately, establish what you need in your life.

Start with time. You, like everyone else, have 12 months, 52 weeks, 365 days, 8,760 hours, and 525,600 minutes each year, regardless of your age, income, or location. You have the same amount of time every year, regardless of how well you used your time the previous year.

Because everyone starts at the same place, the difference maker is how you use your time and where you focus your attention. I don't believe in a balanced approach. "Balance" suggests that everything you do needs equal time, which is a misguided notion that sets unrealistic and unachievable expectations. You may think if you only work harder on your time-management skills and focus on building super human capabilities, everything can have the same balanced attention. It's just not a worthy pursuit. This type of thinking sets you up for failure and disappointment.

Instead, think about how you can integrate what matters in your life. By establishing your priorities, you can manage how much time and attention you want to spend in each area. Then you can set your expectations and the milestones to show your progress.

I simply don't want equal parts of everything in my life. I want to be able to spend time and apply my efforts differently. Some days I am all in at work, and other days I am all in at home. Redefining the expectation to integration versus balance allows me to reset the way I lead my life. And most importantly, it allows me to have a bigger impact and more joy in my life.

I found it helpful to look ahead on my calendar to get important dates marked. The school schedule, birthdays, and vacations were always first. Then I added my key responsibilities and deadlines for board meetings and staff meetings, as well as key business deadlines, on the calendar. By looking ahead, I could see where the pressure points were going to be and work to mitigate them by reconsidering what I really needed to do. Later in my career, as I planned calendars for my organizations, I used this same order. I tried to avoid key personal dates, days off of school, etc., so others could enjoy their families and friends too.

I remember one summer when our boys were ten and fifteen; it took two hours to lay out our summer schedule. Who was picking them up? Who was dropping them off? But the time was well spent. Instead of scheduling on the fly every day, we had a plan of action. We were able to respond to issues and still keep everything on track. We had less stress, so we could enjoy our time running around and focus on what mattered—being engaged in our life as a family.

A proactive look at the road ahead ensures you provide the right kind of leadership to allocate your time and then hold you accountable to follow the plan. Left without a plan, you'll get submerged in the activity of the day with little regard for what matters. Instead, if you self-direct according to your priorities and expectations of progress, you can optimize your time.

Because days consist of minutes, making small adjustments can be significant. Thinking about time in three time periods is helpful. Always start with the big picture, regardless of the time frame. Then break it into chunks. I think about it as "the Now" (thirty days out), "the Next" (ninety to one hundred twenty days out), and "the Future" (one year and beyond). Having a big picture view and managing your time in chunks helps you align your work today for what comes next. When you run into new developments, having a big picture view and plan allows for more flexibility in choosing a path and moving in the direction that achieves your goals. Remember, you can always control the direction, just not every move. Learning to keep this perspective keeps your options open and you always moving forward.

Several years ago I launched a blog, www.nancymdahl.com, to share leadership lessons with a broader audience. In one of my blogs, "More Seat Time," I explored the notion of discipline and learning from experience. My younger son, Jorgen, races motocross. I know you're thinking, "Isn't that dangerous?" Don't worry about him. Yes, it can be, but I was the one who introduced him to the sport. I love it, and the track is a great place to spend time.

I love motocross, the people, the competition, the strategy, and the demands that it puts on the riders. What I like best is that you can't fake it. You have to do the work, be disciplined, and be focused to win. There are no substitutes.

When a rider's experience gets better, they win more and eventually move up a class; the new class of riders is better than the previous class so it gets tougher to compete. My son has been a motocross racer since he was eight. His gauge on whether to move up was his previous year, where he finished first or in the top three every time. In this new class, he was in the middle of the pack and he didn't like being mediocre. But he had to go through it to get better. If he wanted to get to the top of the new class, he needed more riding time, otherwise referred to as "seat time," against the better riders in that class. The lessons of motocross can feel punishing to the rider, especially when it's early in the season or when he or she has graduated to the next class and no longer ranks at the top.

These same lessons happen in everyday life; you just don't talk about it as "more seat time." Nothing takes the place of preparation, the lessons learned from experience, and the confidence built by completing the "seat time" to make it happen. There is no substitution, no faking it, and no testing out of it. You just have to put in the time to make it happen.

Then why do you sometimes think you can skip it or cheat the system and learn it some other way? Maybe it's because some of the work is mundane, repetitive, routine, or too disciplined. The headlines of people's career aren't marked by these experiences, but they're the foundations people build to ensure a successful career, even though they aren't often visible to the naked eye.

By learning to spend your time, minute by minute, focused on what matters, you can build strong futures. No one will build his or her ultimate success in a day. It takes "getting more seat time" to achieve and sustain your goals in life.

Along the way, you'll meet many "pickpockets" of your time—those people and things that take your time and add no value in return. The biggest one is all the interruptions. Recently, I read that the average person is interrupted every six minutes, and it takes six minutes to get refocused, which is about 20 percent of your hour, and your whole day, if the interruptions continue. The net result is a lack of focus and therefore no progress. Organize your time and tasks to minimize interruptions. Optimize your highest priority items to the most productive hours of your day. As I discussed in chapter 5, you're at peak productivity only a few hours a day. Identify your peak productivity hours and schedule this time to maximize your ability to impact your work versus filling it with surfing the web, sending emails, organizing your files, etc. You still need to do those types of tasks, but don't do them during your peak producing hours. You can make a different choice.

Establishing boundaries and routines is important. Only you can do it. Sharing with others what you expect will establish a clear understanding of your routines and boundaries that will optimize your performance and your team's performance.

# INTEGRATING WHAT MATTERS IN YOUR LIFE

Over the years, communication has moved from the Pony Express of the 1860s, when sharing information took time and money, to today, when almost everything is faster and free. In the early days of communication, you were able to send your communications based on the priority of the message. The things that mattered most were either faxed or sent by an overnight delivery service. Everything else was sent standard mail. Today, the priority of the communication gets lost because everything is sent instantly via text, email, and even Snapchat. Not all responses need to be instant.

I have found it important to establish a standard practice about when I'll check messages. By clearly communicating my standard practice, it sets expectations about when people will most likely hear back from me. Then if they need a response more urgently, they can let me know in other ways. You likely already do this when you go on vacation or attend a conference. You indicate in your email auto reply that you'll be away and have limited or no access to email, specify when you'll be able to respond, and if there is an issue, how to get a hold of someone else. Extend this standard practice to the rest of your life.

The practice of learning to understand boundaries and then using them to allow you to optimize you is a powerful tool. Boundaries can range from how you manage your personal space, to what you share about your personal life, to how you interact with others. They can include projecting a clear understanding of the different roles in your life, as well as how you manage the accompanying accountabilities and responsibilities.

Years ago, boundaries were easier to understand because organizations and cultural traditions created many of them. Both the boundaries and the expectations were clear. For example, in my hometown, everyone's weekly schedule was pretty well set. Sunday and Wednesday night was for church, boys' sports were played on Friday nights, and girls' sports were played on Tuesday and Thursday nights. Our family calendar was dictated by my father's work, with the exception of our family's obser- vation of holidays and special occasions. Everything else moved to fit his schedule. There were expectations about what was acceptable behavior for girls and boys, what were proper dating rituals, what dressed up and casual meant, and how we talked to our elders.

Today, these social norms are no longer true. Everyone moves to his or her own beat, and boundaries have become blurred. Left with no clear boundaries, people are subject to others' interpretations, which are based on their needs—never a winning formula for being your best. Establishing your own boundaries allows you to build a "mojo" that optimizes how you integrate the various areas of your life.

But even with well-established boundaries, integrating what matters in your life isn't easy. Life isn't a harmonious experience. It's fraught with tension that requires you to make tradeoffs and prioritize what matters most. Sometimes your priorities compete for the same resources at the same time, so it forces a choice. Integrating your goals with the allocation of resources—time and money—requires a different approach.

As I discussed earlier in this chapter, living an integrated life, but not a balanced one, is possible. One day you may be all in for your work and another all in for a family vacation. In a balanced world, there would be a winner and loser each of those days. But in an integrated life, there are no losers, and the reality of these demands is incorporated into your daily life. Over time, you achieve your goals in both work and family areas, as long as you manage your time well.

> *"Instead of wondering when your next vacation is, you ought to set up a life you don't need to escape from."*
>
> *—Seth Godin*

Your perspective on how to integrate your life will change as you move from your twenties to your sixties and beyond. Initially you may be focused only on your career, physical fitness, and friends. As your career and family situations change, your focus will be significantly different. I'll explore this concept in more depth in a later section—"Sharing My Top 10 Life Lessons."

# 12

# CHARTING YOUR PATH

*F*inding your career path in the world is hard. Taking the time to understand who you are as I've explained earlier in the book gives you both the freedom and courage to identify and do the work that leverages your strengths and complements your weaknesses. Notice I said leverage your strengths and complement your weaknesses, not eliminate your weaknesses. Everyone has both. The important thing is to focus on how to make the full package work to optimize you.

Today's culture loves to point out weaknesses. It's as if by drawing your focus to them, somehow they can be eliminated. I simply don't buy that approach. Instead, I believe that you'll get growth where you put your effort. You can become acutely aware of your strengths and weaknesses so that you can be intentional in managing to your strong suits, although eliminating your weaknesses isn't possible. Everyone has weaknesses. You need to live with them and learn how to manage your total self, weaknesses and all.

As you work to chart your path, remember that you're never growing a business or a career. You're living an awesome life that has a career in it. You should only be working on being the best human being you can be. If you do that, the result will help build your organization and your career.

Whether people publicly admit it or not, everyone is in some stages of forming or charting their path for their careers and lives. The process is a lifelong pursuit. As your road winds through your life, you benefit from the miles that you've traveled. Sometimes, the beginning is the hardest because you don't know where to start. However, the same may be true later on when you meet a fork in the road. In the end, you'll be in the best position to make good choices if you have committed to the lifelong discipline to build your self-awareness.

Sometimes, people can get a jump-start by working for organizations that push them along in their development programs. You can be fooled into thinking that because your organization hired you, it will define your career path and what you get to do at each level. Each level will have a prescribed time frame for advancement, an HR or training department that will nurture your advancement, and a recruiting industry that prescribes what a successful career looks like. But that isn't reality—those days are gone.

Today, you are on your own. I would contend everyone was always on his or her own. Some people landed in organizations that operated with prescribed career paths that helped them find their way. Some hid behind this programmatic approach and marked progress solely against it. Others took it as a guideline and continued to "drive their own bus," prescribing their own career paths, timelines, and objectives.

You are and were always on your own.

Being on your own feels uncomfortable to some, maybe even unexpected. After all, your formal schooling more than likely had expectations and a prescribed time frame. In high school and earlier, the path was largely the same for everyone, with some opportunity to choose classes and majors, but with the same timeline for everyone. Post–high school had a larger variance. Some individuals finished in the standard timeline for their programs, whereas others took longer or some chose not to even take a post–high school program or don't finish.

After you start a career, the variances are even greater. Gone are the days when you worked at one company for your entire career. Today the dynamics are wildly different. Over the course of your career, the average person reportedly will have seven to ten jobs. For those people just starting out, the new likelihood is twelve to fifteen jobs.

The volatility in the job market is due to economic instability, the change in marketplace dynamics, and the increased autonomy of workers. Learning to be intentional in your planning has never been more essential to your future success.

In fact, four in ten people are likely to be working independently by 2020. Standard career paths for the masses will morph into something that looks more like individual mazes. Technology's impact on how people can work, the globalization of the workforce, and a new definition of how individuals want to work drive these changes.

Just like everything else in the world, work is moving from a standard approach and look of success that's the same for everyone to individualized plans that bring meaning to personal lives. The paths will be less obvious and more adaptable, and thus will be a more accurate reflection of what is important to each individual.

The twenty-first century will be a time when the hard work you've done to learn who you are and what you really want out of life and your career will matter most. It will favor those who choose to live with intention—same facts, different experiences, on purpose. Your ability to acquire skills will be important, because what you learn in schools or companies won't keep pace with the rapidly changing world. Your learning laboratory will be real life. Your ability to practice how to debrief in which I talked about earlier in chapter 3 will create the agility to move forward. The debrief process will allow you to unpack your learning from your experiences and build a better you—someone able to connect the dots that matter to you.

I love the quote from Alvin Toffler of *Future Shock* written in 1970. He said, "The illiterate of the twenty-first century will not be those who cannot read and write, but those who cannot learn, unlearn, and relearn." His insight almost fifty years ago to forecast what would be important is impressive. Your journey will be to learn the habit of self-awareness, which will make it possible for you to live your life aligned with who you are every day.

The company and the job become your stage from which to practice and build your skills. Your job will be to make you so invaluable that your company creates roles for you that reflect the path you have chosen to accomplish your version of success, not the other way around. You live in a broader world than just your company, so don't limit your thinking to the boundaries you know.

It's easy to say, but hard to do. As you gain momentum in your career, the trappings of your success can easily seduce you. Your success will make you feel great, so you continue to give more and begin to compromise other areas in your life. If you get a promotion, the momentum to fall in love with your success will build. Slowly your identity gets wrapped up in both your job and your company, and you can't separate them. I've already shared the story about how my career success caused me to lose touch with my family and life priorities. I had to alter my path to build a strong family. Work will never tell you to go home and will always have more for you to do. Work also won't come see you when you're sick and in the hospital.

Work isn't the complete definition of you. Keep this distinction clear. Your focus needs to be how to integrate your whole life. I've talked about the importance of this perspective several times. An integrated life is a healthy life. You need to be disciplined about living an integrated life, so when you're off course, you can take steps to make a correction.

One day when discussing this topic, a friend equated our importance to our organizations as a fist in a bucket of water. When you pull your fist out, there is no hole. The hole just fills in and continues to be the same bucket of water. The same is true of your roles in your organizations. Of course, you can build a reality in your own mind that makes it impossible to imagine that anyone could replace you and do your job. The fact is that they won't replace you and all your attributes, but your organization will fill the void. Life in your organization will continue without you.

## The Chapters of Your Life

No one has a plan for you; you must create it on your own. Build your plan from your foundation and think about all the options you may have to achieve your goals. Smaller segments help the process.

In the beginning, I thought about my whole career and life. Now, I think about my life in chronological chapters, the length of the chapter varies depending your life stage. This perspective makes the process of thinking about what lies ahead both easier and way more fun. I don't worry about all things anymore. I stay focused on only what is important right now and put my future ideas in the appropriate future chapter. Then I don't lose them and can consider them as I approach that time frame.

I have also found it helpful to come up with a name or theme to guide me during each of the multiyear chapters. It helps me be clear about what the goals are in this chapter and creates urgency to stay focused because each chapter is time bound. My goal is to have the current and next chapter named. This gives me time to think about the third chapter. As I move along, it becomes clear what the theme needs to be for that part of the journey.

When I look back in history, my chapters varied in length to fit what was going on in my life. For example, my high school chapter was four years and the same for my college years. Then, as I started my professional life, I had an eight-year chapter for my early career named "Just Getting Started." It included my first job; then changing companies three times, moving four times, getting married, and building a house; working part-time jobs to earn extra money; living with several housemates to give them a jump-start; finishing my MBA; and supporting my husband in grad school and launching his business.

The next chapter, themed "Taking It to the Next Level," covered seven years and focused on making all the parts of my life work together. That point included a growing family, two puppies, momentum in my career, and my husband's decision to focus his energies on the construction industry, specifically in sales and design, which are his passions. His business had grown, and now his energy was largely consumed by the administration of running the business. He wanted to return to his roots.

For the next ten years, the chapter was appropriately themed "Living an Integrated Life." We worked to be engaged in our family and build strong relationships, experiences, and traditions, as well as to build an executive career for me and a thriving business for my husband. We also became more involved in our community. My husband was coaching sports, and I had new board work for me.

Just as people start their leadership roles from different places, the same is true about being intentional with your life. For some, being intentional is natural, and they start in the beginning with this perspective. For others, the thought is new or is something that they may have known about but never had to think about because life just happened. Then when life doesn't happen, at least the way they wanted it to, they feel stuck, scared, and maybe just a bit terrified. I've seen this reaction from recent college graduates who need to figure out their next stage in life, as well as career professionals who experience change later in their lives.

The feeling of being adrift plays a number on you and starts that conversation in your head that likes to tell you what isn't going well. Most everyone has had them, but you always feel alone when it's your conversation. You know the times . . . when you leave college and are really unsure of your future. When you are in a job you don't like. When a significant relationship ends and your world changes. When a job ends due to a downsizing or maybe your own decision and you don't know what's next.

Your ability to stay focused on what you know and to find the next move is critical.

Forward movement is progress and needs to be celebrated; just don't put your bus in park as you decide what to do. Drive around a bit while you figure it out.

During this time, people lose their courage to continue in their quest of an intentional life. You may ask, "How can I be intentional when this stuff happens?" Being intentional is about declaring your direction and continuing to stay focused on your overall goal—it's not about believing that you can control every move. Regardless of how good you are, things happen that you didn't expect. Your focus and center of confidence needs to be your keel that gives you the stability to make forward progress in the direction that is important to you.

> *"Success is never final and failure never fatal. It's courage that counts."*
>
> *—George F. Tilton*

As you think about what is possible, seeking out opportunities that develop you at each step of your process, regardless of your title or company, is key. Don't limit what is possible by some imposed boundary. Or don't be convinced that you need to eliminate your weaknesses. Your focus needs to be on how to optimize your gifts and your contributions in amazing ways. Learning to seek opportunities that embrace you matters. The best part is that you can be aggressive in seeking opportunities to contribute from wherever you are. Those opportunities can come from being part of a task force, special project, or community service, or dedicating time to create your own apprenticeship by working alongside others.

Part of getting the opportunity to be involved is asking. If people don't know you have a desire to work in this area, they may not think to ask you. By taking the first step to let others know or by offering to help, you'll practice your ability to be intentional and move the ball forward for you. Then the relationships you make, the work you do, and the results you bring to the team will open more doors. You just need to start from wherever you are and go as far as you can, and then you'll be able to see farther, which makes the next move clearer.

The opportunities you chose will fit because they piqued your interest and you felt it was worth your time and energy to learn more. Sometime they come your way because you put yourself in the lane to be considered. Others will come your way because others thought they fit what they perceived you needed next. Still others will come because you were curious and open to discovering something new.

The final choice is always yours. For me, the best learning opportunities were the ones that had the magic four ingredients: variety of challenges, intensity of effort, diversity of settings, and adversity of conditions. There are no shortcuts to authentically developing yourself. Years of experience aren't a good measure of your ability because ten years in the same role can be one year of experience repeated ten times. Learning to pursue opportunities that expand your experience and include all or most of the four ingredients matters. Even if it is in the same role, expanding the depth and breadth of your capacity is critically important.

Developing your skills and abilities should be a primary focus in each new opportunity. Learning to more fully understand your foundation of your "you facts" (refer to chapter 6) and your self-governance of what you believe and what you know is critical to unlocking the full potential of your future experiences.

The key skills to develop in the first five to ten years of your leadership career are understanding command skills, mastering conflict management, learning creativity, managing and measuring work, motivating others, building a broader perspective, and learning to plan for a bigger scope.

As you move to jobs that are larger in scope, you'll want to focus your energy on dealing with ambiguity, managing innovation, negotiating, developing political savvy, demonstrating strategic and organizational agility, and managing vision and purpose.

## Barriers to Advancement

Sharing my perspective on why some people don't advance is also important. This is the flip side of the previous discussion and allows you to more clearly see the consequences of not developing your skills in key areas. Over the years and many conversations about leadership that I've had, the people have changed, but the issues preventing them from moving forward in their careers share similarities. One of the biggest reasons people don't develop their skills in key areas is the inability to learn or a lack of understanding of others. When I would find myself in a conversation about someone's career and look at his or her track record, a lack of self-awareness and curiosity was obvious. I saw it so often; it was one of the reasons that eventually led me to write this book.

Beyond this primary issue, it should be no surprise that the other issues on the list include the following: inability to adapt to differences, unwillingness to accept personal learnings, defensiveness, overdependence on a single skill, political missteps, failure to build a team, betrayal of trust, insensitivity to others, and key skill deficiencies. Most if not all of these issues stem from a lack of personal understanding and curiosity. So learning to be diligent in building your own self-awareness as a life skill is essential. Building the debrief skill and using the framework I discussed in chapter 3 will build the muscle that allows you to optimize your future experiences more fully.

Knowing this list is important. It provides a perspective for you to consider as you gather feedback about you and your leadership. Can you see evidence that any of these areas need special attention? How are you doing at developing your skills in each area or how are you guarding against these career stallers?

One of the most difficult exercises is to find the target areas for your development. There are so many areas. Where do you begin? As with anything, understand the context of skill development as well as how the skill requirements change as the scope of your job grows.

I found the Leadership Architect® tool by Lominger International to be helpful. The tool develops life skills regardless of your profession and does a fabulous job of helping you understand how the skills are related and how they cascade from basic to advanced. The organization, Lominger International, has done tremendous research in this area to help you focus on key development and strength areas. In fact, its Leadership Architect Diagnostic Map allows you to see the correlation of the skill to the level in an organization as well as the degree of difficulty. It has been helpful for me to see the progression of skill development so I can focus on an appropriate skill now and then anticipate what is next.

Remember my multiyear chapter example? Knowing what you need in each chapter now allows you to focus and not get preoccupied with all the other things that you'll need for your future. This ensures a stronger foundation so when you add the other skills later, your foundation continues to build strength versus experience cracks, which happen when you don't finish the work of developing the skills needed earlier, so when you add the weight of the next layer, your foundation crumbles.

Then think about how long you want to be involved in each stage, opportunity, or event. When will it be time to move on? Think about it: elementary school, middle school, high school, college, graduate school, your first job. They all have an ending. Funny how you can learn it in one part of our lives, but you don't translate it to others.

This question is important to ask at the beginning: "When will this expire?" or maybe, "Under what conditions will this expire?" The question helps you bring clarity to what you expect and maybe more important, why you're doing it. The clarity makes it easier to see the signs that tell you that the end is near and make it harder for you to build a different reality that only exists in your mind.

Refer to the discussion where I explained about mapping your life's events in chapter 8 and 9. Look at the detail you wrote about when you transitioned to a high point or a low point. Did you see a pattern? Look again at your work. By recognizing the signs of change, you'll be more proactive in seeing the transitions coming long before they arrive. You can also check in with your goals to see if it's time to move on or to recognize that the situation won't change, so your relationship with it needs to end.

The hard part is that some opportunities come with a clear expectation about when things end so people know what to expect. Sometimes they even plan for it with big fanfare. Others don't, so the ending surprises them. They feel the sense of loss more deeply and more personally.

Change in your life is inevitable. The only unknown is whether you'll let the change happen or be proactive in managing the results. Not that you can plan for every ending, but you can expect things won't last forever. Learning to begin with the end in mind will be hard, but it's worth the effort. Declaring the expiration date at the beginning will ensure that your "why" and "for what reason" are clear and will create an urgency to do your best work before the time is up.

Isn't that what leading your life is all about?

# SECTION III: LEADING OTHERS

**Time to Raise the Bar on Your Leadership . . .**

Leading your personal life is one thing. Leading others is quite a different thing altogether. To be clear, I define leadership in terms of how someone acts, not by the position he or she holds. All individuals have impact on others in the way they live their lives. Does your impact make the world a better place?

This is the first of three sections to examine leadership of others. The best leaders understand themselves so they can focus on others. Self-knowledge is what this book is all about, and a clear understanding of self has a profound effect on the people in your workplace and family.

Self-knowledge is hard work and takes practice to do well. As you move on to leading others, this same skill can help you understand your impact on others. In addition, you can examine how others lead to gain new insights that can shape your leadership. None of this work is very sexy, but it's vital to being a high-impact leader at any level.

> *"When the best leader's work is done, the people say, 'We did it ourselves.'"*
>
> —*Lao Tzu*

# 13

# CROSSING THE THRESHOLD

*A*ssume that you've decided to take on a leadership role. Doing so is a natural next step. To really optimize the opportunity, stop and think about what this really means and why you want to take on this role.

First, what does it really mean? Leadership is about people—other people. Leadership is about influencing and mobilizing people to achieve a common goal. Leadership doesn't exist until you create a relationship with another person. Your relationships drive the result and actions that you seek.

Pushing for efficiency to accomplish your goals is a great pursuit. However, leadership is rarely an efficient affair. Leading from here to there is almost never a straight line. I talked earlier about the power of emotions. The people in your life also have emotions, feelings, and history, but many times they haven't spent the time to truly understand themselves, which requires you to pause and help them understand themselves first so they can be focused on their own personal development and not getting in their own way. This results in short-term inefficiency, but ultimately drives great value because you're working together to discover issues and solve problems.

I know from experience that better outcomes don't always mean doing something faster. I also know that the easy way isn't always the best way. Looking for shortcuts to drive a straight line of results can cause you to miss a lot. Many times, the crooked path adds depth and color to both your personal and work life that you can't get any other way. Holding another meeting, having critical conversations, and reinforcing commitments, principles, and values can seem like a waste of time, especially when you see the goal and clearly need to get moving. But if you don't take time to do these things so people know who you are, you may end up on your own—leading no one.

Good relationships, cultivated over time, will bring you the level of commitment you want when you need it the most. If you haven't taken the time to build relationships, all you have is a stick. From my early days growing up in a small town, I learned the power of relationships. I've made it my goal to build relationships that endure time. Some of my most trusted advisors have come from my dedication to first building an authentic relationship and then practicing the discipline to stay in touch.

As a leader, your primary responsibility is to put people in their strengths zone where they can leverage what they are good at to do their best work. So spending time to get to know your team is important. If you hired someone and he or she isn't getting the job done, you have only two possibilities:

- You hired the wrong person. You didn't take the time to understand his or her true knowledge, experience, skills, and motivations.

- You hired the right person, but *you* are in the way. You're either too hands-on in doing his or her job, leaving little room for the new employee to learn and grow, or you aren't teaching him or her the additional skills to truly excel. How does this happen? Well, you may not be transferring your knowledge and experience to the new employee in a way he or she understands. Or maybe you aren't engaged deeply enough to see the organizational structure, attitudes, and barriers that stand in the way of your employee's success. Worse yet, perhaps you aren't seeking a broad enough base of feedback to help you see the full context of the situation, relying instead on your close inner circle of colleagues who are just like you.

Either way, it's your responsibility. You are one hundred percent responsible for the success of your people. Accepting this on the front end will allow you to grow as a leader and not allow you to dismiss your new employees as idiots or incapable of doing the job. You need to stop *spending* time *on* them and focus on *investing* time *with* them, so together you can move forward.

Everyone can all make their organizations and communities better places to work and live, but no one can do it alone. Leadership is about the power to bring people together and deliver a collective result that is bigger than anyone could have done on his or her own. The process is always about $1 + 1 = 3$.

Leadership is a big deal. In the end, it isn't about your position, title, or some vague philosophy. Leadership is a real job that comes with serious responsibilities that have consequences.

If you don't want that challenge or don't want to accept the responsibilities as your own, stop right now and reconsider your decision to cross the threshold from leading yourself to leading others. There is no harm in making this choice. Leadership isn't for everyone. Society unfortunately pushes people to seek this role as a marker of success. The biggest harm comes from accepting a leadership role because you like the status, perks, or the story you can tell without the commitment to accept the responsibility.

Leadership means having the humility to accept the responsibility for the decisions you approved, for better or worse. Projecting decisions onto your team members to insulate you from the responsibilities of a leader isn't a winning formula. Most people can give examples of leaders they've worked for who do just that. Making the commitment to lead with intent is about knowing that it's your responsibility to be the role model and to show what's possible for your organizations and your people and not follow the rut made by others.

Leadership means that you'll have to push aside the notion of acting like a boss—dictating orders, focusing on the negative, being the sole source of answers. This is a notion rooted in the leadership dark ages of the industrial revolution in the late nineteenth and early twentieth centuries. The quest solely focused on producing things, and workers endured whatever conditions made the things possible. Fast-forward to today, when many of the traditional barriers are gone. Leadership now favors the individual and environments that are friendly, supportive, collaborative, and fun.

I love this quote from Thomas Friedman that I have already used in this book: "If you are self-motivated, WOW, this world is tailored for you. The boundaries are all gone. But if you're not self-motivated, this world will be a challenge because the walls, ceilings, and floors that protected people are also disappearing. . . . There are fewer limits, but also fewer guarantees. Your specific contribution will define your specific benefits much more. Just showing up will not cut it."

Selfish behavior by a leader damages the organization, and inconsistent behavior, from good to bad and back again, is possibly the worst condition of all. The carrot/stick metaphor is simply not good for business. Workers are more likely to forget the carrot and remember in perpetuity the stick. Leaders who practice this kind of management are a direct reflection of how they feel about themselves.

A good leader has the ability to model the personal touches that can make such a tremendous difference in the work environment: the ability to show respect for each other, to acknowledge and embrace others' perspectives, to embrace personalized approaches to getting the work done, to express appreciation for forward movement, and to get constructive feedback and learn together. These human touches are what fuel the belief that the people you're leading are personally supported and someone actually cares. In return, people will pursue the mission with all they have to give.

In the end, driving successful change and sustained performance begins with your own self-awareness and then embraces the same concept for others. Learning to pause and continue to build self-awareness in you and in others is an evolving process critical to any leader's success. A recent research study by Korn Ferry showed that companies with employees who were self-aware outperformed employees who had a lower self-awareness. In fact, poor performing companies were 79 percent more likely to have lower self-awareness among their employees. Optimizing your results is impossible unless you fully understand your individual and collective capabilities.

This research, with its hard evidence, builds the business case for self-awareness, which is the most crucial developmental breakthrough for accelerating personal leadership growth and authenticity. The value of knowing yourself is that you leverage your potential. The process provides clarity about your strengths, so that you can assert them in the appropriate circumstances, and your vulnerabilities and weaknesses, so you can keep them in check and work to prevent you from asserting them inappropriately and in nonvalue-creating ways.

When you're self-aware, you move in touch with reality; people trust and respect you more. When you aren't self-aware, you abdicate your responsibility to know your strengths and weaknesses to others and lose credibility and the ability to lead.

## Why Do You Want to Be a Leader?

One of the most important questions to ask yourself is why do you want to be a leader? Is it because you like the title? The pay? The social status? If those are your reasons, you'll never be a truly great leader.

You need to understand your purpose as a leader. *Harvard Business Review* reports "fewer than 20 percent of leaders have a strong sense of their own individual purpose. Even fewer can distill their purpose into a concrete statement." But if you take time to identify and define your purpose, you'll become energized. Your enthusiasm will be contagious. You have the potential to become a great leader, not just a good one.

Remember earlier when I talked about understanding your personal mission and how powerful it is to giving you focus? The same is true here—except this time it focuses on your leadership.

In the end, you should be able to articulate the following:

I want to lead (<u>company or function</u>) that gives the employees (<u>benefit to them</u>) and results in (<u>overall goal</u>).

Leadership is about people and collective results. Your leadership purpose needs to answer the question for you, the people, and the results. The focus on people will keep you anchored. If you ever lose sight of your team members simply because numbers are getting in the way, then you have a major problem.

Only leaders who know what their own purpose is and who focus on the people who work for them are the ones that move from the category of good too great. They take their roles far beyond management and truly fill the chair of a leader. These leaders are also the ones who take the helm of an organization and generate such great performance from their team that the organization or company can't help but succeed.

My personal story here is taken from observing some really poor leaders who impacted the people around them negatively. I observed people I worked for who focused only on how to make themselves and not their team members better. They only cared about and focused on how stellar their individual contribution would be.

The moment I became the leader I am today was when I moved my focus from me to others and helping them do their job better and to be their best self, both personally and professionally. Although it was some time ago, I remember it like it was yesterday. I was leading a business that served a geographically diverse field organization. We were working our way through some thorny issues that required a broad view to ensure that the solution optimized the business results for everyone. My job was to lead the discussion, encourage discovery, and guide the team to a final solution. The outcome was less about what I did and more about how the process caused others to take action. In the end, we tackled the situation and executed a plan that was a win-win for everyone and allowed us to build momentum across the organization. My ability to work across the organization allowed me to build relationships that are still part of my life today.

The focus on building my team members into their personal best heightened the quality of my relationships in ways that I can hardly describe. The people had clarity about our purpose and what we were working for together. This clarity allowed my teams and divisions to move with me on the journey to reach our organizational goals.

# 14

# BUILDING YOUR LEADERSHIP MUSCLE

*E*very leader starts in a different place. No one walks into the workplace with all the skills required to manage a team, inspire people, and grow a business or organization. It takes an ongoing focus on building your leadership muscle. Just like an athlete works to develop the muscle to compete, through practice. The same is true of your leadership muscle.

Your first job as a leader is to understand your team, first as individuals and then as a group. Understanding what is possible today and the potential for development is critical. Just as you did the work to understand you, the same is true of your team. Understanding the gaps in your team's professional development is essential to determining if changes need to be made to optimize your results.

What does leadership need to look like for both your individual team members and the group? How do you, as a leader, need to engage to stay in tune and fully understand where extra attention is needed and what people and activities will succeed with little oversight? As a leader, you're charged with making the news, not just reporting the news. If something isn't working, your leadership is where the course needs correction—either to accelerate progress or take a time out to debrief before moving forward.

Certain transitions have to take place to allow you to elevate your game. Building relationships is foundational but not sufficient to being a great leader. Being successful as a student, programmer, salesperson, engineer, marketer, project manager, or any other position is no guarantee that you'll be adept at managing others. The experience and skills are important, but your talent—your natural recurring patterns in the way you think, feel, and behave—really predicts where you'll perform your best. The work you did in mapping your life in chapter 9 gives you a glimpse at what these patterns look like for you.

Gallup, a well-respected research organization, reports that the best leaders have the following talents:

- They motivate every single employee to take action and engage employees with a compelling mission or vision.

- They have the assertiveness to drive outcomes and the ability to overcome adversity and resistance.

- They create a culture of accountability.

- They build relationships that create trust and open dialogue and full transparency.

- They make decisions based on productivity, not politics.

Gallup's report indicates that only one in ten people can master all five of these requirements. But with the right development plans and coaching, organizations can improve the impact of 20 percent of their high-potential leaders, resulting in a 48 percent higher profit.

People are simply too valuable to waste under a leader who doesn't get it. Time and again, I've seen extremely bright, high performers who haven't had the chance to add value because their leader's focus wasn't on building the team's expertise.

One of the clearest examples I've encountered of an undervalued employee came when I joined a company in a vice president position. I had a direct report who had extremely poor performance reviews. Everything I had heard about him from the people who worked for him were things like "He yells at us," "He's caustic," and "He focuses only on the numbers."

When I met with him for our first one-on-one meeting, I sensed his desperation. His division was struggling, and he was trying to achieve the expected results. He felt pressure to bring in the numbers, so that was his major focus.

I decided to challenge him—I asked him all types of behind-the-scenes questions about what was going on, and I questioned his approach to solving the problems. We worked together for more than a year, and then we planned a regional meeting where I asked him to use a new set of problem-solving approaches.

He led the meeting, and I was a guest. His leadership took command of the group from the very moment he welcomed the audience from the stage. He took time to introduce himself and explain why he was passionate about the company mission. During his talk, he shared a story about his sick mom and how he had been taking care of her. His visuals and the details showed a more complete picture of who he was, first as a person, and then as a leader. It had a profound effect on his team. The entire division had a new understanding of whom this man was—caring and focused on family. After this meeting, his division rallied around him and achieved the numbers and results the organization needed.

The point here is if I had taken the information and opinions from his other managers, I probably would have fired him. His previous managers failed to get to know him as an individual and instead focused only on the numbers, so he was leading based on what he saw in others. Through observation, he had been taught that there was no time for relationship building and that he should focus just on the numbers and the results would come. When I encouraged him to use a different approach, he learned that when he took time to make connections, people would feel he cared and unite around the mission because they believed in each other.

The leader who understands the power of teamwork focuses on creating a vision for the team with clear objectives and priorities, establishing clear roles and accountabilities for each team member, delegating effectively, listening to feedback, and collaborating to achieve bigger results. This is particularly important during transitions—when starting a new project or tackling the new year's business goals, for example.

Remember, leadership is about people.

Your job is to organize the work of other people, so collectively you can perform at a high level. If you aren't clear about where you're going and what your expectations are, if your people don't feel valued in what they can contribute, you won't get the results. Delegating the work doesn't mean passing off work you don't enjoy, but it means letting your team members stretch their skills and decision-making abilities.

One of the best ways I have found to work with others is to take time to pause at the beginning stages of forming a team to understand what each team member knows. I ask each person to share the special talent or gift he or she wants to bring to the project. That way, I can leverage the knowledge and experience of the group from the start. Taking time to build this context helps everyone understand the vision and how he or she is collectively accountable to each other. It also keeps the focus on the project objectives versus all the other noise that can come into play.

Communication is another important aspect of team leadership. Your communication responsibilities are to your direct reports, your boss, and the entire team. They all matter. Don't try to take shortcuts and only focus on your boss; doing so won't motivate your team. On the other hand, don't lose sight of the importance of communicating upward so your boss is in the loop and not surprised. Your boss can also be a great resource to gain new insights and a broader perspective.

I have found that communication snags have been the reason for most, if not all, of the issues that have ended up on my desk or pulled me off task. For example, if people don't know some of the facts, they often fill them in with a negative version. They can pass this negative version to others, often as the truth, with additional negative interpretations added along the way.

How do you deal with this? First, try to reduce the chances of it happening in the first place by sharing all the information you can, as you get it. Second, if it still happens, address it as soon as you can. The pace of the world today doesn't give you the luxury of time or having the complete picture before you need to take action

Learning to build the muscle to be disciplined in this area will allow you to progress and fill in the new information as you move along. Focused communication drives connection with your team and key stakeholders. Poor communication will erode trust, which is a fundamental for all leaders.

Your communication plan should include progress reports and debriefs on what you and your team have learned so far. Doing so allows you to get everyone on the same page and together. This will ensure that everyone is with you. I have found that real-time updates are the best way to learn out loud with the team. They shouldn't be big formal presentations, but rather quick debrief sessions that keep everyone on the same page and make it clear that you're holding the team to its individual and collective accountabilities. You'll feel like a broken record sometimes. Keep in mind that everyone processes information in different ways and speeds. If you have said it once, say it again and in multiple formats.

**You Simply Can't Overcommunicate**

Finally, your role as a leader is to set the pace, be open about not having all the answers, and demonstrate your courage to make timely decisions. Yes, you're rolling up your shirtsleeves and working with your team, but sometimes your role as a leader also requires you to push others to move faster. Sometimes, you need to break the work down so you can move it in smaller pieces, allowing everyone to see and feel the progress. Each step will bring you to a bigger goal. Be clear about when the work needs to be perfect and when good enough is good enough. Your early progress can build steam that makes the next steps move faster, allowing you to solve issues on a more manageable scale if things don't go as planned.

The easy way out for leaders is to declare the organization can only cope with so much change, but in reality, both individually and collectively, the organization longs for progress. Slowing down probably isn't the right answer—you'll lose momentum. If you feel you have hit this point, communication and celebration of the work done so far is probably what you need, not a slower pace.

One of the most challenging communication situations I have dealt with was a turnaround—where my team and I had to facilitate change across an entire organization. The change involved the entire matrix of the company—not just the silos—and how we worked together as a community.

We had spent a great deal of effort on several change initiatives. At the end of the quarter, everyone was tired and burned out. People were asking to take a break and to take a quarter off before our next change phase and return to business as usual.

Instead, we took one day. Friday came, and we organized a closure meeting to acknowledge the work we had done. Gathering together to recognize the enormity of what we had accomplished in the last quarter and celebrate our success helped us reignite for the next phase of the journey.

After the closure meeting, we went to dinner. For dessert, I ordered one of everything. This practice has become one of my trademarks. I like the smiles it brings and the guilt-free tasting experience for everyone. For me, ordering one of everything is also a metaphor for building teams. Each dessert has its own special brilliance and individual ingredients unique to that dessert. In the same way, each team member brings his or her own special brilliance to the team. We share dessert together to celebrate the unique differences among our team members and how, together, we collectively contribute to the success.

The team members took one day off from work—the following Monday—and then we returned to our change initiatives for the next quarter. Communicating our successes, our vision, and our steps for the future reenergized us and helped us continue moving forward through the planned phases.

Your reaction to feedback and ability to stay resilient will set the tone for the team. Proactively reach out to people with different interests. Seek input from the broader group so you're certain that you're aware and engaged. You can help break the logjams if you're in the mix. Don't wait to hear a problem or success reported at an update session. This leadership process is simple to write on paper but includes lots of nuances in practice.

In chapter 6, I talked about how to hold your own debrief sessions to help you identify and understand what is affecting your outcomes. I encourage you to revisit the practice of debriefing often as you pause to reflect on your impact as a leader. Isolate the noise that clouds your ability to see reality. Pay particular attention to the filter layer.

The courage filter is what separates average leaders from great leaders. Courage, which can also be referred to as confidence, is a more important asset than skill, knowledge, or even experience. Without confidence you'll find it difficult to make tough decisions, be proactive, lead meetings with authority, persevere through adversity, get people to communicate with you candidly, and be open to feedback, particularly difficult messages. Without confidence, you'll second-guess your decisions and find yourself defensive when challenged. Without confidence, you may find yourself sadly lacking in one very important component of leadership—followers.

Never underestimate the vital connection between leadership and confidence. People are more willing to invest their time, energy, and loyalty to ensure that you and the team are successful when they feel your confidence and trust you. Revisit your work on your centers of confidence in chapter 10. Then do something every day to boost your confidence. Doing so will build a habit that makes your impact life changing.

The price of admission to move into a leadership position is your ability to deliver results. To stay and advance in your leadership role, you need to develop your ability to lead people who can do the same thing.

# 15

# PUTTING YOUR NAME ON IT

*Nancy M Daly*

In my hometown, I was the only Nancy Johnson. When I arrived at college, I was one of five, so I learned to use my middle initial to ensure I received my mail. Using my middle initial became my initial point of difference and a practice that I continue today. With a simple Google search, I can see that more than 7,000 people in the United States have my full maiden name and almost 100 people have my married name. Learning to establish your point of difference and identity is important.

The work of your team members begins to build your brand as a leader. Expectations move from what they know they can expect of you as a person to what they can expect from a team under your leadership. Your natural tendency may be to treat team leadership like a group project in school. Chances are you were the one who did the extra work to make up for those who didn't pull their weight. People wanted to be on your team because they wanted a good grade.

But that approach doesn't work as well outside of school. Too many times, I see people get stalled or frustrated because they aren't advancing. These people are almost superhuman in the amount of work they do, but they fail to develop the people below them. As a result, they see higher turnover rates and find that their people aren't sought after for advancement. In many cases, no one wants to work with them because they're just too difficult to work with. They don't embrace the talent of others and find collaborating as part of a team or across the organization difficult. Their lack of confidence gets in the way of learning to delegate, to hire people smarter than themselves, and to receive constructive feedback.

As I advanced in my career, I would get calls to see if I had any openings on my team. And every time I made a move to a new team or organization, I received the same type of calls from the people with whom I'd worked. The word on the street was, "If you are on Nancy Dahl's team, she will build you both professionally and personally because she expects you to add value. If you don't want to be pushed to transform yourself into the best version of you and learn to add value, Nancy Dahl isn't the leader for you."

The cool news about my approach to building a team is that it almost always guarantees that the best people will seek you out. They want to be pushed, make a contribution, get their hands dirty, and make an impact. They like that you have high standards and won't keep the dead weight on the team. They don't want to be micromanaged, don't want to follow orders that give them little room to make the work their own, and don't want to be blamed for the failures and given little credit for the success. In short, your job is to be a conductor, not a controller.

> *"Leadership by example is the only kind of real leadership. Everything else is dictatorship."*
>
> —*Albert Emerson Unaterra*

Here is an example from my career. I had just been promoted to a vice president role in a new division. I knew the assignment was tough, but the start was simply awesome. Two weeks after I started, I had to travel to Cabo San Lucas, Mexico, for the midyear meeting.

I must admit I was a bit nervous. I didn't know many people in my new division, which was under fire because the sales and profits weren't meeting expectations. The new COO and I had worked together previously, but we had never been in the same division. He liked my approach and wanted me on his team. He knew I liked to win and that I believed in the front line and would be engaged to drive the results. He needed that to turn the division around.

When I was initially approached about this opportunity, I turned it down. The original job spec had focused on maintaining the status quo, not playing a major role in reinventing the division. I knew it would be a mismatch. I am a terrible maintainer. I get bored. I had no interest in the promotion if I could not see an opportunity to make a difference. To be clear, that meant setting new standards of performance for the team and frankly, the industry. That's what gets me up in the morning. I didn't want to accept a position just so I could get a title and all the perks. For me it was about providing leadership that would impact people and deliver the results.

As I prepared for my presentation and to make a connection with the people in my new division, I knew speaking to their heart was critical. I told my personal story through my photography of my boys. At first, I felt that being so vulnerable was a risky move. This was the first time I had been so transparent about who I was, what was really important in my life, and how it applied to our work at the company.

I was wrong about the risk. Making myself vulnerable was exactly what was needed.

The sharing of my personal story made a huge difference in how the team members connected with me. We created an immediate bond, and the openness allowed us to connect on a personal level much faster. Our journey ahead became one built on trust, intense focus on the mission, and a shared commitment to do what was needed to turn the division around.

I know my presentation was critical to achieving this, but a fishing trip might have also helped launch this connection, too.

I love to fish. When I arrived in Cabo for the meeting, one of the first things I did was book a fishing boat for six. I had no idea who would join me, but somehow that didn't stop me. I just knew I needed to fish. I offered the opportunity first to my direct reports. WOW! All the places filled. Later, we learned that another group from our division had booked a second boat. The competitive banter about who would do better began. We finally made a bet for most fish, biggest fish, and first fish.

I'm happy to report that after lots of smack talk, our boat won all three competitions. Everyone caught fish. My fish was nine-feet long and 190 pounds. That night, we had our fish for dinner. We noticed that the other group members were in the restaurant, too, so we had a plate of our fish sent over to their table so they could enjoy it, too. What an awesome way to celebrate the day. The replica fish on my wall still brings a smile to my face. The fish will forever be the marker of an awesome journey that we had as a team, as well as the birth of my individual discovery. I learned that I needed to connect first with the hearts of the people, so I could then connect with their heads, and finally, get their hands busy.

This experience set the stage for our journey ahead. We were behind sales forecasts and needed to act with urgency. We launched a road rally campaign to get everyone focused on what they could do to drive a different result. Slowly, we built momentum. The results were published every Monday at ten o'clock. If they were late, I got calls. Everyone knew how his or her results contributed to the team's overall goal. We were aligned on our goals, felt supported to do our jobs, celebrated our progress, and took time to share feedback so we could learn together.

As you build your leadership discipline, you'll see how this type of engagement allows you to continually gauge your confidence in the team's ability to deliver and be proactive in your leadership rather than having things happen on your watch. By delivering consistent results, you can build a reputation as a can-do leader that others can count on.

# 16

# PREPARING FOR THE UNEXPECTED

*O*ver the years, you're taught to prepare—for tests, projects, and special events in an effort to get the right results. You learn that it isn't acceptable to be unprepared with your answers, presentations, or approach. Sometimes, presentations or answers feel like you're learning the lines of a play that need to be perfect for opening night. You're terrified about the consequences of not preparing.

As a leader of you and others, demanding that everything be anticipated and planned for is misguided at best. The unexpected always happens, and you and your team need to be ready to optimize new opportunities or make course corrections when new situations arise. Rigid planning is one of the biggest challenges leaders face today. A prescriptive approach can lead you to think that you're making progress against your plan, when the world has changed and you're now off course from reality.

In the previous chapter, I talked about a new leadership role I had taken and how I learned the importance of connecting with the people to drive results as a team. Three weeks into that assignment, my boss showed up in my office early one morning. We were both early risers, but we weren't scheduled to meet. Something told me this wasn't a check-in visit. He was on a mission. He asked me to commit to a $1-million-dollar increase in sales in the second half. I paused, and then told him I would figure it out.

I was three weeks into the job, but I was up to speed on the fact-finding I needed to do when tacking a new situation. I knew that the incremental sales he was looking for had never been done before and that no evidence showed the current trends would support such a move. However, I reminded myself why I was brought on—to lead change and create a new reality.

I accepted the challenge and brought it to my team members. I acknowledged that I was asking a lot, but I expressed my confidence that we could achieve this together. We started with the right spirit, and the challenge became fun as we worked together to figure it out as we went. We knew that no one had the answers, but we were confident that we could figure it out. We focused on just a few metrics and set ninety-day milestones with frequent debriefs to accelerate our performance as a team. In the end, we delivered a $1.7-million-dollar increase, almost double what we had been asked, all because we had the trust and connections with each other and believed we could figure it out, even though we had no idea how.

## Learning to Be Comfortable with the Uncomfortable

Things happen that you don't expect. You encounter things for the first time. You experience feelings that you didn't anticipate. There are simply too many combinations of situations to be fully prepared ahead of time. When faced with the unexpected or uncomfortable, the trick is to say, "I will figure it out," instead of "I'm not prepared." By building your confidence and agility to figure it out, you can always be prepared.

I first experienced this early in my career. I was at the office late, and I was frustrated. My pile of work that was "waiting to hear back" from someone was growing. In an effort to get the ball rolling, I decided I would take a different approach. I looked at each project and wrote down my answer to the open issue and sent it off.

The next day, the people I had been waiting for started responding. Forward movement! Even better, as the responses to my answers came back, I learned two things. First, most of my answers were dead-on.

Second, the ones that weren't right could be corrected on the fly and didn't affect the quality of the overall work. In fact, we were back on track and not rushing to meet deadlines.

Coming up with an answer and watching new answers come back bolstered my confidence as a young leader and pushed me to move more boldly from that day forward. The value of this approach is one I still use today with my teams. Your school years teach you that someone has the answer book and you need to work to get that answer. Real life usually has more than one answer and not an answer book to reference. Forward movement relies on your ability to solve problems. Sometimes, you just have to make it up to break the logjam.

Yes, I said, "make it up." Making it up allows you to move forward and relies on your leadership and good judgment to make the right choice. What I have learned is that 85 percent of the time I'm right and the other 15 percent can be corrected on the fly. Of course, I would never recommend this when dealing with safety or regulatory issues or matters of life and death, but in most other situations, it's a perfectly appropriate choice.

Making it up also frees your people to apply their thinking and problem-solving skills to the issue. It promotes resourcefulness, personal accountability, collaboration, and teamwork. Making it up makes it okay to say, "I don't know," but keeps you on the hook for using your good judgment to move things forward. As you review project plans, someone might question certain aspects of the plan as he or she seeks to understand. Sometimes the answer is, "Well I just made it up." That almost always brings laughter. I have also noticed that saying "I just made it up" accelerates the team's learning and quality of work and gives them permission to "make it up" at appropriate times as well. In the process the team develops a new view and a list of new possibilities that were there all along, but no one was seeing.

Try saying, "I just made that up," sometime. It has amazing effects on people and their ability to get work done. In the end, this process makes the work more fun, brings new energy, and makes your team members feel empowered to do their best work. Keep a careful eye out for those individuals who don't feel comfortable with this approach. They don't want to do it wrong. They want to get it right. You may have to practice with them as they try it and make it their own. Doing so will be worth your time to help them work through it. For some who only want to operate with black and white rules, you may need to add making it up to the list of rules so they can see you mean it. Allowing your team members to make it up frees them to change the way they're thinking, so the focus goes from "I don't want to be wrong" to an energizing exercise of "What else could I do?"

In helping teams deal with the unexpected, I have also found it helpful to ask questions, such as "What if we didn't want [that] to happens? What would we change to have a different outcome?" The questions help change the perspective when you're pondering an issue, and it appears that you're stuck. The questions stop people from starting to go down the path of "poor us" and "Why does this happen to us?" Posing a forward-looking question focuses the team's energy on a solution instead of moving backward to regurgitate what is wrong with the situation.

By embracing the issue and its complexity, you can lead the group through the thinking together and bring it to an outcome that the group can do something about it. Through this action you demonstrate your ability as a team to figure it out—a critical competency to compete in today's world.

# 17

# BUILDING A STRONG TEAM

*I* have this vivid memory of arriving to work on my first day as a new leader. I was twenty-three years old, just six months out of college, and only three months into a new job. I had been promoted to a supervisor position in a new division of the company in which I worked. I was assigned to an area that had two small teams of four people. Only one of the eight people was close to my age; the rest were older. In fact, one of the team leaders was more than twice my age. I was excited to be in this area because I could use my marketing, business, and communications degrees, but I was worried about whether these two teams would accept me as their leader or just tolerate me.

As the days progressed, I learned more about my team members' individual jobs, our overall accountabilities, and the importance of building strong relationships with our field offices. Since I had lived my life under the rule of work first, play later, work is where I focused. Everything else was secondary. This approach wasn't new to me. I had done it while growing up too.

As a supervisor, I took special care to keep my conversation only on work and to leave my personal life at home. I arrived extra early and stayed late to ensure that everything was done and I was on top it. The supervisor of the other teams did the same thing, so I felt like this approach was the right way to do things.

In the end, I did gain their respect despite our age gap and built a solid relationship with them that was more personal and authentic than the previous supervisor. However, while I had successfully used a work-comes-first approach in high school, college, and even on this first job, I realized that learning to be a good leader was so much more than working hard night and day. I could see this was a shortcoming of the previous supervisor and the VP of the division I was in. I needed to unlearn it in order to achieve an integrated life that wasn't just about work.

When I left that company and was promoted again, I learned the importance of sharing more of your personal story. This too was a learned response, and something I had to unlearn and relearn. I grew up in a small town where everyone was in everyone's business. In college, I enjoyed building some separation from my small town story, and I liked it. I thought it made my life easier.

At work, I couldn't see the value that sharing my personal interests would provide in getting my job done. I thought it would just get in the way. What I missed by carrying forward this old belief was the power in sharing who I was as a person so my team could relate to me on a personal level. My personal story was the missing link in allowing a relationship to be built.

My job as a leader is to help team members succeed. If your team members feel good about their contributions, are trusted and respected in their workplace, and believe that you care about their success, their work will show it. In chapter 8, I talked about the importance of having a leadership mission or purpose statement. Your people need to know your purpose statement as well as your values, philosophy on leadership, and your role. You need to be clear about the behaviors and principles that guide your work and those of your team. You need to make it clear how to work with you and what you expect from them.

Learning to share my inside story of whom I was as a person allowed me to engage with more authenticity with my team. Up to that point, I was only focused on the outside story: my titles, education, community leadership, academic achievements, and awards. I thought my outside story mattered the most. I didn't want to let anyone see the inside story because I thought my personal story would get in the way. Boy, was I wrong.

The inside story is what draws a team together. I didn't really understand its power until I was forty. During an annual meeting, I shared a personal story to illustrate the power of a brand. My story featured an image of a Harley rider dressed in leather with a baby in his arms. The stark contrast of the tattoo on his big muscular arms and the tenderness of the baby created a powerful image. As I continued to talk about the importance of building a strong brand, three big guys walked on stage dressed in leathers and stood to my right, which drew the audience into the story. I finished my speech that day by telling everyone I loved to ride motorcycles, too. I had been riding since I was just nine years old and still enjoyed the sport. In fact, I told them that I want you to meet the guy who taught me to ride, my dad. He was one of the three guys standing on stage. The audience erupted with applause as the riders walked off stage and handed company tattoos to the crowd. When they left the auditorium that day, we had three really cool motorcycles on display. Seeing the crowd gather to take a look and talk with the riders was fun. It has been more than fifteen years since I told that story. And still to this day, I have people ask me if I have been riding lately.

After your people understand who you are from the inside, they get engaged more deeply, share their talents more fully, and can work side by side with you, focused on accomplishing a shared mission. I felt better working this way, too. It was at this point in my life I committed to building a life that feels good on the inside, not one that just looks good on the outside.

As I worked with my team members, I checked in and asked for feedback and listened. Listening allowed me to learn more about their perspective and the work, which in turn allowed me to see where my leadership needed to add value that would help them do their best work. In the end, I found ten common themes or expectations that my team had of my leadership and me. Here is what they asked of me:

- Notice me and understand what I can bring to the table to help drive results.

- Trust me and explain the big picture rules so I understand; then give me the freedom to do my best work in a way that works for me, supports the team, and delivers the result.

- Support my career goals and help me integrate my work and life goals.

- Connect me to the overall vision so I can understand how my work makes a difference.

- Include me as a productive member of the team.

- Challenge me to be the best me by giving me feedback and challenging me to bring more discretionary effort to the role.

- Encourage me to learn from my mistakes, be a sounding board in difficult times, and help me build confidence in my ability to make a difference.

- Hear me so I know that my input is considered.

- Laugh with me so we can have fun. It's okay to be silly and poke fun.

- Recognize me when I do something well and say "thank you."

Learning to connect with the individuals in your organization is what makes you real to the team. It's also what makes it possible to engage in their work more deeply. This list of ten team needs has been a focus for me regardless of the scope of my responsibilities. This list doesn't cover some of the finer nuances, but it's a great general rule to begin to build a strong foundation with your team.

# BUILDING A STRONG TEAM

## Looking Back

In retrospect, this perspective would have been helpful earlier in my career. I could have done a better job of engaging with the group and been a better leader of both myself and for others. I wrote the two chapters earlier in the book regarding the power of debriefing (chapter 3) and the framework (chapter 6) to help you accelerate your ability to be more intentional than I was early in my career. Building your self-awareness and confidence will allow you to engage with others in a more meaningful way so your leadership will drive a bigger impact sooner in your career.

The second part of building your team is getting to know your team members and building a sense of what you need in a team to do your best work as a leader. Individual team members should look different from you—different, yet complementary—so they fill in the holes/gaps in your skills; add a diverse perspective, yet are capable of supporting an overall goal; and have the courage to make contributions even when they have a different idea. In end, the team delivers 1 + 1 = 3 every time.

What exactly do I mean by "different but complementary"? Consider these key points. You aren't looking to build a team that's just different. You're looking to build a team of diverse talents that have the ability to accept their individual differences and understand that their job is to support a collective focus. Building a cohesive team that can operate at this level is critical.

Initially, I didn't understand the importance of building a strong collective team focus, and I made the biggest hiring mistake of my career. I hired a very talented and accomplished professional who came highly recommended by a close friend. However, this person wasn't capable of allowing different opinions and embracing a collective focus unless the collective focus was a confirmation of this person's opinion. Because a diversity of opinions wasn't allowed, it destroyed the team. This leader nullified and devalued others' ideas. Because of this person, I lost some extremely talented professionals who previously had reported to me. It hurt.

I chose to skip a step in the company standard recruiting process and didn't do the industrial psychology review because this person had a competing offer. I thought I knew enough, I felt it would work, and I skipped a step, which came back to bite me. Hiring is one of the most important decisions you will make—don't take shortcuts. Be thoughtful, timely, and thorough in your process. In the end, hiring is still a risk, but if you take care up front, you can catch the things that won't work.

A leader's capability to handle diversity is of utmost importance. Allowing you to do your best work is vital. But if you aren't ready, at least understand yourself, so you understand what different but complementary means. Be clear about what role each person plays and do the work to ensure that those individuals you bring onto the team understand their collective results are as a team and not only as individuals.

As a leader you must be engaged with the team members as they learn to embrace their differences. The team may be designed to work with you, but not with each individual member. Building a functioning team with the right mojo requires you to have the right alliances to harness the team's collective strength. Your team needs to know your focus is on working with people who drive results. Decisions about who to bring onto your team are critical—they're likely the toughest decisions you will make.

**Important Questions to Ask about the Future**

As a team leader, keeping a careful eye to the future is also imperative. What do you see? What will be required of your team in the future versus now? Is your team capable of evolving? If not, what changes do you need to make? What do you need to do to make sure your team can develop to hit the demands? The questions about the future work keep your team relevant. Your job is to do the work to build the perspective on the future. Your team is counting on it. Don't skip a step and take the easy way out by promoting the status quo in what has been done, because it has worked before. You must prepare for what is ahead, not just ride with the way things have been done before without careful consideration of what will be needed in the future.

Your leadership will grow in value as you demonstrate your ability to build strong teams. Your team will be the place others come to get candidates for promotions and a place of joy for you as you watch your team members stretch and grow into their full potential—all because they had a leader who believed in them, long before they saw what was possible.

# 18

# LEVERAGING YOUR FRAMEWORK

*I*n the first section of the book, I explored how to take ownership of your life and build strong self-awareness. In chapter 3, I introduced a debriefing framework that was designed to give you a systematic approach to learning more about you and how to evaluate feedback. At the risk of repeating some of the same topics, I want to pause to highlight the importance of developing a habit of using this same framework to help you as a leader.

When you move from an individual contributor to a leadership role, things get more complicated and the feedback starts to get filtered. In a large part, because you're in a new role, people may not be frankly candid with you.

Some people will filter their feedback to you because you're now in an influential role. They want you to see them in a good light so you can help them achieve their goals. Others may filter their feedback because they consider you the competition or someone who is different and doesn't fit, or because they don't like what you're doing. You represent a threat to them personally. Their best interest is to give you feedback that is less than complete or at least not supportive.

Being different is sometimes exactly what they say they want. But when you arrive and bring your skills and talents to focus on the very thing they said was important, you may find out they didn't really mean what they said.

A big part of your job is to build this process of using the framework to collect and evaluate feedback as a habit and a competence that becomes second nature, and then work to build a broad base of feedback. When you do both, the disconnects become apparent and you become more proactive and are able to see where you need to do more work to get the real picture. The feedback process will also build your confidence by giving you a clear picture of what is going on, which will make you less vulnerable to being blindsided by personal attacks.

The feedback framework will help you build a broad base and an independent evaluation process, allowing you to be engaged in the right issues at the right time. Without the full context, you can easily chase "red herrings"—those things that appear to be the issue but are only a distraction from what matters. This causes you to lose valuable time and leadership credibility.

When you truly dedicate yourself to the discipline of building a strong, diverse base of feedback, you will learn to see things from many different angles. You'll see where others may disagree with you or are withholding information from you. When I would follow up on feedback to ensure I understood, the people were always surprised. Because they're usually isolated in their own encampments, they don't anticipate that you would talk to others and learn of possibly negative feedback.

As you work to gather, observe, stay engaged, ask questions, and be curious, you'll collect many impressions. You can easily end up relying on a few trusted people. Although getting feedback from a few is efficient, it's rarely the best approach. Remember, we as people see others as we are, not as they are. Even if your trusted advisors are reporting the facts, impressions, or feedback, expand your network of feedback sources.

People give you feedback based on their perspective, which means it's subject to their own personal bias, cultural norms, and prior experiences. Don't assume that they've done the work to understand their own bias. You need to work to understand their language and perspective so you can make the appropriate interpretation for you.

Another important aspect to note is that by nature, when people know two facts, but there is a gap in between, they always fill it in negatively. You need to work to resist this natural tendency and always fight to fill in the gap with what you actually know, not what you think or assume.

Because your role as a leader is to work with people to achieve results, you're going to run into issues that get created from the human experience. To address these issues, you need to build a leadership competency of reconstructing the facts of the story so that you can focus on the issues and not the people. That way there aren't any losers, only a winning team. Leaders who walk their talk earn a reputation of trust, respect, and authenticity. That, in turn, will enhance your team's commitment to you and the results you desire.

# 19

# SITTING IN THE "OTHER CHAIR"

*I* could tell this employee was upset. The urgency of his voice when he called was the first sign. When we met, I could see the signs as I watched him walk toward me, the stiffness of his shoulders, and the expression on his face.

We sat down, and he thanked me for taking time to meet with him. I thanked him for reaching out and taking me up on my open door policy. He was a bright, take-charge person who liked a challenge and exploring new ways to get things done. He was involved in a major initiative to transform the business, but he had hit a roadblock.

I listened as he explained the situation. He reviewed the project plan and its major milestones and gave context to the impasse. I asked questions to slow the conversation and bring clarity. We took a deeper dive into the situation. To him, the next steps were so clear, and he was frustrated that others didn't see it. In some cases, he felt that others were abandoning the work.

We spent our time talking about why this might be happening. It was a big change to the business model and the impact was starting to show up. Although the project plan outlined the change process, it couldn't predict everything. We talked about the need to slow down to ensure that everyone was brought along.

I asked him if he had sat in the "other chair." He looked at me with a question on his face. I explained to him that a project lead can easily see things from only one perspective. Sitting in the chair of others lets you see it from their perspective. The sides will ask questions based on their perspective. At times, they can appear to be selfish, not supportive, or counterproductive. But the questions they ask are really important. The answers help bring understanding to an issue so individuals see their role in the overall mission. Without a personal understanding first, change efforts can't be supported globally.

We talked about how this might be the case here. We identified where the work needed to be done to have the right conversations and gain a better understanding. He left my office with the commitment to do the work and follow up with me at the end of the week.

On Friday, when I turned the corner to enter my office, I could see the furniture had been rearranged and something added. A sign "the other chair" was taped to the back of the chair and a thank-you note was on the seat. Three days had passed since we had talked, and the project was back on track. It's funny how taking a break and changing your view can give you the perspective to break the logjam.

Learning to develop the ability to see things from the other chair is vitally important. Remember, you're wired to see things are as you are, so creating a different view takes your intentional effort. As you build urgency to take action, you reduce your ability to see the alternatives or to really listen. These habits help you build this broader perspective.

First start with the perspective that in life there is never only one way to do things. As a leader, your job is to work with your people to accomplish results. Learning who your people are and how they work will put you in a position to understand their perspective more fully. Practicing the art of asking questions to flush out what you know, what you think, and what you believe, either as a group or one-on-one, is time well spent—even if it doesn't feel that way at the time. It allows you to hit pause for a moment and lets everyone recalibrate before you hit play again.

## Seven Blind Mice

From time to time I have used unconventional ways to illustrate this point. I love the children's book written by Ed Young, *Seven Blind Mice*. The book illustrates the issue of different perspectives in a fun way by sharing the diverse responses of these blind mice when they, one by one, investigate something mysterious by a pond. They each come back with a different theory, because each has only explored a small area of the something. "It's a pillar," says one. "It's a fan," says another. It's only when the seventh mouse goes out and explores the whole something that the mice see the whole truth. In essence, the seventh mouse sat in all the "other chairs" in order to come back with a solution.

This book is a great way to ease the tension and get people to look outside themselves and sit in the other chair, so in the end they can work together to accomplish their goals. It also reminds me that everyone can make his or her organization a better place, but nobody can do it alone.

As you work through a situation with your team, focus on the issues, not the people involved. When you focus on the people instead of the issues, the discussion becomes personalized and prevents forward movement on the overall goal. It sucks energy away from the team, deflects accountability, and sidetracks the entire team. Your job is setting the right tone. Make it okay for your team members to share their perspective, admit what they don't know, share what isn't going right, and offer alternative solutions.

When things don't go as planned, allowing time to discuss the reality of the situation in a timely fashion will allow you and the team to focus on solutions versus wallowing in what went wrong.

# 20

# REFRAMING THE DETOURS

*R*egardless of how you prepare and plan your life, things will happen that weren't planned, both good and bad. What differentiates you is how you process the event.

Sometimes you'll see a reaction that suggests the detour was just a bump in the road. Other times, it will cause people to stall and almost completely shut down. A death, a divorce, a loss of a job, a demotion, not getting a job applied for, a stalled career—are all major life events that can significantly affect people emotionally and in how they live their life. Remember, people are feeling animals that think. The power of your emotions will impact your ability to stay focused.

The detours challenge your resolve to live your intentional life plan. The detours will make you rethink this notion of choice and control. Is the experience real or a figment of your own reality? Lastly, the detours push you to reexamine the work that you've done to identify your "you" facts—mission, values, strengths, weaknesses, accelerators, and derailleurs, as well as your goals and your self-governance—what you believe and what you know.

Reexamination isn't a detour. In fact, reexamining is what allows you to move forward and not wallow in the aftermath. The work is hard, but worth the effort because it moves you forward and gives you new insight. Sometimes the new insight pushes you in a new direction, because you have a new perspective. Being disciplined to reexamine your current understanding allows you to add depth and ensure your future direction makes sense. In some cases, you'll unlearn and relearn, and in others you'll add new insight and texture to something you already know. The net result is a truly grounded foundation so your plans stay in alignment with doing your best work. The foundation ensures that you remain strong and confident even when things don't go as you envisioned. It brings clarity to the question, "Am I here because of where I came from or because of where I'm going?"

In the end, what you do with the new reality after the detour matters. That's when you work to build your future or decide to stop. I love the saying, "Life is 10 percent what happens to you and 90 percent what you do about it." You learn leadership as life happens to you. Although you can learn ideas in books, how you act and react in the real world builds both your competency and capacity to lead. Your ability to understand the meaning of leadership grows as experiences happen to you over your lifetime. The quickest way to learn about an aspect of leadership is to hit a detour or make a mistake. As long as you take the opportunity to learn from it, you can build your capability to improve.

Except for the effects of a death, which has its own process of working through the loss, the debrief exercise is a valuable one to walk through the unpacking of the event (see chapter 3). All four of the questions of the debrief process are important for you to answer, but the third one sometimes is the most revealing: "Knowing what I know now, what could I have optimized better if I were to do it over again?" When you examine the situation with hindsight, you look at alternative ways to optimize your result. The third question prompts you to ask "what if . . ." and proceed in a forward-looking direction with the benefit of 20/20 hindsight. This requires you to optimize the situation versus to replay it over and over again and dig a rut. When I have done this, I have seen how my personal actions, leadership, and overall preparedness could be different.

I also recommend revisiting the 4 Rs (Recognition, Reflection, Reframing, and Responding) in "Getting Past the Emotional" They help you break through the emotion and see a situation with a more rational mind. The 4 Rs have allowed me to identify when a situation is untenable—where I couldn't do anything to fix the situation. When this is the case, it begs the question, "What choice do you want to make?" Do you stay and do less than you know should be done, but keep the security of a job, a relationship, or a routine you know? Or do you forfeit the security and pursue your dreams and desires? Now to be clear, you can come to the latter decision and not leave, but rather begin your process to secure your next stage of your work and your life. Either way, know that you'll never be successful with people who don't value you and your contributions.

Let me be clear that this choice—to stay or go—is yours. Both require thoughtful consideration. Both require you to know why you're choosing to make that decision.

If you stay in an untenable situation, be aware that you unlikely will feel fully engaged or as inspired by your work as you once were. You need to reset your expectations for staying, or over time you'll grow miserable and part of you will die. You'll lose your enthusiasm for your work. Your path will be challenging unless you have another place to put your passion and world-class work.

I have faced this stay-or-go decision on several occasions. Everyone does, at some stay in point, I'm certain that you've met people who have chosen to stay in a job or relationship they clearly don't like. They often feel stuck, because they have forgotten that they always have a choice, but that choice requires they do the work. Their emotions have them stuck, building ruts that seem impossible to change. Your life is too valuable to be wasted in jobs or relationships that don't optimize you. Don't ever trade the thrill of living your life with the potential to do your best for the security of existence.

*"Never argue with stupid people, they will drag you down to their level and then beat you with experience."*

—*Mark Twain*

Sometimes, I chose to stay and look for other opportunities within the same company, such as a new boss or a new project assignment. However, I also did an evaluation and set a time frame for how long I would stay to see if anything changed. In my evaluation, I identified what changes I needed to optimize me. The evaluation created urgency for me and yet gave me time to think everything through to make certain this course of action was right and not just a reaction to a highly charged emotional event. The extra time allowed me to gain a new perspective on another way to move forward. Sometimes, this alternative was there all along, but I didn't see it because I was focused on my way or what I knew. Taking a step back after you have done your debrief gives you time to move forward, while looking at your new conclusions to ensure that you haven't missed anything. This step is valuable to build your confidence that your plan makes sense.

When you choose to take a different path and seek opportunities where doing your best work is possible, you need a new approach. Using the debrief process, you must turn your focus to think past your current boundaries, turn your fear into faith, generate original ideas about what is next, explore new options, and rationally think through the obstacles. This focus fuels your ability to live with determination and won't allow you to get sidetracked or de-motivated. It also allows you to be unshaken by your critics and naysayers, because you know you're doing the right thing.

Reactions from your critics are important to consider in your evaluation. They help you to plan your own change-management process to take you from Point A to Point B. Not everyone will embrace your new reality with the same enthusiasm, especially if you're in a long-term relationship or a legacy business with family, or you have ownership in your business. The feedback and reaction you get are a result of how your change affects them, not by how it serves you. Taking time to think through how others will receive your change allows you to manage your emotions and stay in your "wise mind" space, which we explored in the chapter "Getting Past the Emotional." It is your sole responsibility to make decisions and optimize you while managing the relationships responsibly.

## REFRAMING THE DETOURS

As you gain clarity about your next move, you'll feel your energy build. When you focus on being a master of your destiny, you reignite your passion and zest for living your life and find the determination to work through the issues that may arise along the way.

# SECTION IV: LEADING FROM THE C-SUITE

**A View from the Top . . .**

Organizations large and small, for profit or nonprofit, all share the need for a C-level leader. This includes a Chief Executive Officer (CEO) or Chief Operating Officer (COO), as well as other C-level leaders. Sometimes organizations have both a CEO and a COO, and sometimes they are combined. Either way, the roles they play are important for any organization. Their leadership drives the focus and resource allocation for the organization and sets the tone for how the work will be done.

I remember the first time I was offered a COO role. The CEO/chairman of a former employer of mine was working to reinvent the company. He asked me to return to replace the COO of a division where I had led change before with great success. I accepted the opportunity because it gave me a chance to make a difference, bring a renewed focus to the value proposition, and drive alignment in the organization to optimize the results.

I had a strong foundational knowledge of the organization's culture and the people who worked there, so I didn't feel the need to do any due diligence or investigation into the role. I'd worked at the company before and felt pretty comfortable I could step in and make a difference, especially because the leadership was excited to have me back in the organization.

I quickly learned that my role as COO was drastically different from my other senior-level leadership roles. I had to rethink the way I communicated. Now I was not only communicating a division's progress, but I also was communicating more broadly as an entire organization. I had a learning curve, but I didn't take long to figure out what was required.

Since then, I have been fortunate to be in a C-suite role for three different organizations. Each time, regardless of my due diligence, the issues arrived faster than I wanted, and typically, arrived in the wrong order. The level of complexity was higher than expected and so was the pace.

This section gives insight into the demands of a C-suite position, regardless of the organization's size. It provides my unique perspective as someone who's occupied several C-level roles. The section also will give you both context and examples to help you imagine how you might perform. Here I look at how it really feels and what it takes to take a chair in the C-suite.

# 21

# ASCENDING TO THE C-SUITE

*I*t took twenty-six years, fifteen jobs across four organizations, and a whole lot of tenacity before I was offered my first opportunity to lead an organization at a C-suite level.

I will never forget the conversation I had with my boys when I came home and said, "I have a new job! I'm the new COO." Their follow-up questions were "Do you get a bigger office? Do you get a sweet parking spot?" They made me laugh.

For the boys, it was important that I answer their questions, as silly as they seemed. But frankly, in a C-level role, where your office is or where you park your car doesn't matter as long as you're leading your team to do its best work. I wanted the boys to understand this perspective, too, even though I didn't bring my work home with me often.

I've always maintained a solid boundary between work and home. The boundary gives me a space to relax and escape the pressures of work. In addition, the status of what a title may bring has never driven me, although I strive toward the highest levels of performance for my teams and me. A title is always temporary. The results of your work are what matters. I work hard to understand front line pressures and never assume my position holds more prestige than that of the frontline employees.

According to a McKinsey Global Survey, the most successful executives who move up or over to a new C-level position share these characteristics: they communicate priorities, value their team's wisdom, spend enough time on culture, and understand their unique leadership role. In the end, your role is, first and foremost, exemplified by the ability to lay out a clear vision that defines what you're trying to accomplish and what the achievement of those goals will mean to the business. Running a close second is the ability to inspire others to do the work and accomplish the results.

When I look at the major news stories, what stands out is a crisis of leadership. When you look at the underlying issues, the problems usually point to the key elements of the framework that I talked about in chapter 6:

- The lack of key elements in your personal filters—courage, risk, conflict, communication, and curiosity.

- The lack of personal self-awareness—your you facts.

- The lack of ability to build value-added relationships and hold both you and others accountable.

The importance of the individual leader's self-awareness goes hand-in-hand with the organization's self-awareness. An organization must be grounded in the reality of its strengths and weaknesses and its needs and issues to choose its initial priorities—what will and won't continue. Many organizations may be able to articulate what they want to accomplish, but when digging deeper, most haven't done the homework to really understand the realities and implications, and thus, have expectations that aren't based in reality.

Flaws in both the individual leader and the organization are key drivers in the tremendous turnover of C-suite executives. Most leaders can lead when the conditions are right. However, the ones who can rally the troops through rotten weather and imminent danger are true commanders. The leaders who are able to become true commanders aren't smarter than others; rather, they're more engaged in the business, more connected to people, and more supported by the overall company leadership. The components of successful leaders include the foundation of a courageous team, trust, transparent and frequent communication, and the ability to set key milestones and celebrate progress.

The overall support by company leadership from start to finish—including in the middle, when the forward momentum is the toughest—is the glue that makes change possible. The average CEO is in place less than three years, hardly time to drive meaningful and sustainable big change in today's marketplace. In fact, a recent research study found that frequent leadership turnover is detrimental to long-term company performance. Another study indicated that when executives are replaced eighteen months into their new roles, the replacements often repeat the same work as the previous person. Even more important, evidence suggests that foundational infrastructure change takes five to seven years, about twice the amount of time the average CEO stays in the position.

Many leaders seek out the quick fix and have no appetite for the not very sexy work of day-to-day menial tasks that are required to build a strong foundation to support a new future. Many leaders also see evidence of the quick fix in business, government, and in their communities. Sometimes the leader makes big promises, like J.C. Penney's glitzy marketing do-over, which failed to capture the marketplace's attention. Sometimes a company won't allow a more thoughtful leader to take the time needed to make significant change because it wants faster, flashier milestones. Both cases need an understanding of the foundational issues and a commitment to do the less sexy work required to make change happen versus a focus on glitzy claims or making leadership changes solely as a way to indicate progress.

Oftentimes, the C-level executives take the pressure off themselves by not doing the hard work of setting measures to track mid-project progress. Change is messy and big changes take time, especially when dismantling the status quo, setting up new systems, gaining agreement, repairing and building trust, and instilling new behavior. Early stages of change are less visible, but necessary to drive the future. Leading change requires a different perspective and different metrics than overseeing the status quo, as well as strong commitment from executive leadership and the board of directors.

All leaders need to establish a new leadership mojo in which everyone is deeply engaged in the world, focused on the issues that matter, and understand the key drivers of change. Leadership is the ultimate experience model; you have to stay engaged, curious, and willing to admit you don't know everything, so you can learn more to be your best. It means embracing your people to celebrate the work that already has been done and learning alongside them to understand what needs to be done in the future. Leadership mojo accelerates change by making the right connections and alignment that makes execution possible.

Let me tell you about the second COO role I was offered. I had been enjoying a nice meal and a glass of red wine at my company's service awards ceremony. My manager stood at the podium and introduced me as a recipient of a ring for twenty years of service. He told a few nice stories about our relationship dynamics, and then intimated that he knew I'd be moving into bigger roles. I walked up to accept my ring. When I returned to sit down, the people at my table started buzzing. "What did the comment about bigger roles mean, Nancy?"

I had been as surprised by the comment as my coworkers, but I continued to enjoy the evening, brushing off the comment when it came up in conversation. But the seed had been planted, and within a few weeks, I was offered my next COO role, this time for an organization about five times bigger than those I had run previously.

This time around, I was savvier and asked the two questions important for success. My first question to the CEO was, "Under what time frame will you judge success?" My second question was, "What metrics will you use to chart progress?"

I'd learned from my first stint as COO, in a turnaround situation, that one of the most important qualities is patience to push through the hardest moments. I told my CEO, "Let me be really clear—if we have two to three years, the change required in this turnaround situation won't happen. Now, if we're looking at three to five years, we have the time to make true change. It will likely take three years just to truly understand the situation and get the right plan in place."

I considered asking these hard questions as my obligation to both shareholders and employees. I was willing to do the hard work and get my hands dirty, but I knew it would take time. The organization previously had five COOs in a nine-year period. The pattern wasn't one I wanted to see continued. If it did, I knew the turnaround wouldn't happen. After some conversation that addressed my concerns, I took the position.

In the end, it was just talk, because the CEO repeated the pattern of not being willing to act in a new way. It took us about a year just to bring clarity to the issues: the right focus and the right priorities in the right order. Driving real fundamental change was difficult because the desired outcome wasn't grounded in the reality of the business. This environment didn't allow me or anyone else to do their best work. Period. It was clear I needed to make a change.

When I look back, I knew I had been diligent about finding out about all the pieces of the job. I had done my best to put accountability in place, and I could have done nothing to change the outcome. The environment talked about the need for change, but it didn't take steps to act differently to drive change. The learning I came away with from this experience was the importance of setting boundaries between the job and me and learning to recognize when all the ingredients aren't in place to do my best work.

### Conducting a Reverse Interview

When considering a new position, how do you determine whether the right ingredients are in place for you to affect meaningful change? Think about it as a reverse interview. At the same time as I'm being assessed on my ability to take the job, I assess how my strengths fit with the offered role. I listen to both what is being said and what is being left unsaid. I take advantage of this time to ask all my questions and set the stage for my work—if I decide to take the new job or stay in a current job.

When I'm interviewing for a C-suite position, I'm interviewing the leader, too. I focus my energy in understanding these four key areas.

## The Organization's Framework

I work to understand the organization's framework: how the organization works, where its blind spots are, and whether I'm a good fit for what it needs on the team. I ask the organization's people to articulate what they value in their leadership team and what they expect I will add. I question what kind of leader they need for "this time in the history" of the organization. Is it more of the same or is it something different? If the organization's leader can't demonstrate a strong self-awareness, I know I'll be challenged to do my best work because the organization's issues will likely be projected onto me.

## The Organization's Leadership Behavior

Second, I look for patterns in leadership behavior or in the organization's leadership track record in four key areas. I look for evidence that the leaders groom people for advancement, or alternately, evidence of a revolving door. I look for signs of leadership holding people accountable, yet giving people room to learn from new experiences. I look for leadership awareness of organizational competencies—what's there now and what will be needed in the future. For me, the job of a leader means to work with people to accomplish goals and deliver results. People are central to the job; therefore, I look for a strong command by the organization's leader from this perspective.

> *"As I grow older, I pay less attention to what people say. I just watch what they do."*
>
> *—Andrew Carnegie*

## The Organization's Commitment to Learning

Third, I look for evidence that leadership is curious and personally committed to learning—about themselves and about new skills or new ideas. When leaders can't demonstrate activity in any of these areas, they're operating from a teacher mind-set and believe they've arrived and know all the answers. When pushed, they'll likely be arrogant, assuming they know best. It's unrealistic to assume that any CEO/COO is good at everything. I'm still amazed at how some CEOs have built their own reality of knowing best; their pretending makes moving forward difficult for organizations. Understanding where their mind-set is will be important in determining how difficult it will be to make change.

Additionally, I ask them what time frame and what metrics they'll use to judge success and whether they're the same or different from their current practice. I ask them to articulate the organizational support that will be in place to ensure innovation and change can happen and how they personally will work to ensure it stays in alignment. McKinsey reported that only 27 percent of organizations had the right resources and support in place during transitions of C-suite leaders. Resources and support play a key factor in C-suite success.

## The Leadership's Engagement

Lastly, I ask how leadership will be personally engaged in the process. I assess whether leadership relies on their internal network or whether they're personally engaged in collecting a broad range of feedback. I particularly look for any evidence of insulation because I've learned that leading at any level, especially the top, requires visibility. Without access to a broad range of feedback and two-way communication from the organization, the leader's ability to make decisions that are in alignment will be compromised, and I know that this will affect my ability to get results in my C-level role.

When I interview other key leaders in the organization, I look to gather more information about the same topics. This intense information-gathering process creates a broad base of information and data from multiple sources and helps me determine what is real. Of course, the types of questions I ask are different depending on the person, but I focus on hearing and finding similar sets of data around values and leadership. Much of what I gather will be a reflection of the leader from the different viewpoints.

## Preparing for the Demands of the C-Suite

When I first moved into the C-suite, I found preparing for the demands of the job to be difficult. While in many ways I was proficient in my self-awareness and team assessments, I still had gaps of understanding about the new company's business dynamics, culture, and leadership intentions. Especially in my first C-suite role, it took longer than expected to ramp up and be effective as a leader and accomplish my goals. I found myself having to refocus my intentions on my ability to lead so I could be intentional in my leadership rather than leaving things to chance. With hard work, I eventually found my way, but the demands of a C-level job aren't for everyone.

In fact, a recent survey by Career Builder indicated that only 7% of people demand this job. C-level roles require preparation throughout each stage of your career. With each step along the way, you'll find ways to make your preparation more on target for you. When a C-level position comes along, the net result of your preparation is to help you see if you're up for the challenge and if the opportunity is a match. However, even if you're the perfect candidate for the job and the organization, you must also be a good match for the organization's leader. Without a match in all of these areas, it won't work. Take the time to do your homework.

The nature of my first C-suite role required me to lead from a bigger scope where I couldn't touch or see the entire business every day. The role required me to be more thoughtful than previously about where I spent my time.

I thought a lot about how I needed to engage to ensure I set the right tone. The C-title and role naturally create some distance from the people, front line, and real-time feedback. I had to be intentional with my actions to take down these barriers with my people. I noticed my employees gauged the organization's future based on the confidence I portrayed in them and our ability to get the job done.

Learning to be intentional starts with your calendar, because time is your most valuable resource. How you manage time sets the tone for how your team will manage time, so carefully plan it to show others what you expect. I made sure that I examined my habits, particularly where I spent time and why—what were the results I was seeking? If those habits didn't serve my current team and situation, I had to be intentional about breaking my habits, some that I loved. Instead of being in all my old places, I had to determine where my presence was needed most to keep the organization moving forward and plan accordingly. Bottom line, what is efficient and effective for you may not serve you well with your team. By adjusting your time to meet your team's needs, you become more accessible and realer, reducing the chance of your title or position getting in the way.

Sitting in the C-suite, I found clarity of my vision, and my belief in my vision grew stronger. But communicating my vision to the organization was my biggest and my hardest job because it required a tremendous amount of work and time to realize. Believing and communicating your vision allows you to build alignment with your team, which is required and necessary to lead.

Over the course of my career, I have met and worked for C-suite leaders who have given up hope for their organizations and abdicated their role in figuring out the transition to a new future. For me, the C-leader who has given up hope is a violation of the basic foundation of a leadership role. The attitude emanating from the C-suite sets in motion a spiral either in the right or wrong directions.

Seth Godin got it right when he said, "The thing is: failure almost always arrives in a whimper. It is almost always the result of missed opportunities, a series of bad choices, and the rust that comes from things gradually getting worse." I've seen leaders either stay too long or get promoted beyond their level of confidence, and they freeze—and then their actions begin to look like survival tactics instead of actions that take the organization to a new reality.

Sitting in the C suite, I've seen people watch my feet more than my mouth. Never discount your impact. When you're a leader, your presence is meaningful to your team. If you're celebrating a milestone, it adds an exclamation point to the event. Being present also helps you do your job better. As you work around the organization, you can connect the dots and stay agile by spending time building strong relationships and strong communications networks.

In sum, strong relationships and communication provide a strong foundation for building a bright future with your team. The skills I've relied on the most as a C-suite leader are my listening and communication skills, not my intellectual capacity. C-suite leadership is really a combination of being able to use your insight from your previous roles and turning that insight into counsel and collaboration through listening and communicating.

# 22

# CHANGING THE DYNAMICS OF LEADERSHIP

*I*ndustrial age leadership had its place in history, driving efficiency. The factory business model enabled businesses to get the most out of every worker. The expectations were clear, as were the consequences. Employees did what they were told, and then went home. Now, the Industrial Revolution is over. The world is in a new space.

Looking forward requires a focus to unlearn, relearn, and discover new skills. The way business is now done requires senior leaders to remake themselves in the image of the technologically advanced, demographically complex, geographically diverse world in which everyone operates. The greatest barrier to adapting new skills, especially with executives, isn't skepticism about delivering on their promise, but rather their inexperience with the execution. Jumping in is the best way to gain experience. Knowledge brings you potential, and through practice and action, you build skill and mastery.

## Story Sharing

Let me start with the acceleration of story sharing via social media. The human experience is all about being social. It has never been what people do—it's who people are and how they operate. Making connections and introductions and sharing ideas, news, updates, tips, and stories (especially inside stories) are the most meaningful aspects about being human.

I've learned this first hand. One of my passions is photography. I see life through a camera lens and love to tell a story with pictures. For me, photography is a world language that allows me to communicate with others in a compelling way. I capture the events of my family and friends and share these events on Facebook. My story sharing has expanded my circle and allowed me to build relationships with others who share with me our common connection, captured in photos. My social network has grown to expect me to share our common stories, and they, in turn, share my stories with others.

When I started my blog, I initially shared it only with just a few friends. I was apprehensive about putting my blog out there in a big way until I was sure it was right and good enough. Would anyone read what I had to say? What feedback would I get? I went about my blog as planned, keeping the audience deliberately small, until I posted a blog titled "More Seat Time." The blog topic was about Jorgen, my youngest son, and his motocross racing. My son posted it on Facebook, and within several hours, my blog was on fire. This experience pushed me to open my blog to more people and invite readers to participate. After all, what was I waiting for?

Later, I saw the same thing happen with social media when I posted my photography from the weekend or my life events. Within minutes, people responded with comments and requests to be a friend. I started to look forward to this connection after each posting on Facebook. The social aspect extended the number of my connections and built momentum for others to join in sharing stories.

Technology has enabled story-sharing behavior to show up in both our personal and our work lives in a new form and without boundaries. People are now only a few clicks away from making a connection with anyone. As a leader, story sharing also means your customers, employees, vendors, and competitors are only one or two connections away from each other. Story sharing is happening with or without your permission.

I love the change in story sharing and making connections, but some leaders don't. The speed and ease of story sharing and making connections raises the bar on the fundamentals of transparency. Being transparent and truthful has always been the best way to operate, but some leaders add corporate spin to a story to make it more palatable. But the team always learns the real truth, and now the speed with which truth is discovered has accelerated. In this new era, leaders and companies that embrace transparency and who lead ethically with a good moral compass have a distinct advantage.

I remember when AOL first came on the scene. I received a free AOL CD in the mail. I had a friend who was really into technology and the internet. She said, "Nancy, I'm signing you up!" I said, "No, thank you." She wouldn't stop pestering me until I finally gave in and said, "Fine, but I won't ever use it." Boy, was I wrong.

My introduction to AOL was before cell phones and free long distance. This was also a time when I was traveling a few days a week for work. At night in the hotel, I would sign into my computer, and my friend would also be online and we'd chat via AOL. Instead of talking on the phone, we'd communicate through AOL, talking about all aspects of our lives. Chat was really the first form of texting. I enjoyed the connection and conversation with my friend, because it created a quiet space to focus on what mattered in our lives.

My story sharing moved on from AOL chat to emails and then to my blog, which was a more anonymous social interaction and conversation, but one that provided the potential for a wider audience. I then moved to using Facebook to connect and share with family and friends and to LinkedIn to connect with professional colleagues. In the last couple years, I wondered, "Do I keep LinkedIn as only professional connections and Facebook as just personal friends?" I decided the types of communication I share on Facebook are the same types of communication I can and would share with people in my work life. So I merged my professional connections from LinkedIn with personal connections on Facebook. Aside from my blog, I now use Facebook as my main social networking tool, both personally and professionally, though I still keep a presence on LinkedIn.

I found that adding my professional relationships to a personal networking site such as Facebook has broken down barriers. It increases communication opportunities and gives more personal insight to who I am. I was one of the first in my professional peer group to be as open in my professional life via social media as I am with my personal life. It was a huge change from when I started my career. Early on, my peers and I would build our network inside the company, and when we left, we didn't stay in touch unless we had a phone number or mailing address.

These past twenty years or so also have seen a huge change in organizational structure, from a hierarchy model of command and control to a flatter structure that requires stronger communication and connecting skills from its leaders. For me, the transition to a flatter organizational structure was easy. For some of my peers, the transition has been more difficult. When I took my second COO role, I gave every one of my front line employees my cell phone number. My senior-level staff was shocked and asked me, "What are you doing? Do you really want your employees to have unlimited access to contacting you?"

"Yes," I answered. "Giving everyone my cell phone establishes a level of trust between us."

"What if they call you at night?"

"Then I'll know what happened immediately, and I can help solve the problem faster."

At first, I had some problems. My direct reports coached their people on what they could and couldn't say to me. Even worse, they occasionally even reprimanded their employees for talking to me. I took steps to change this behavior by using transparency—making sure everyone had the same information—and by focusing on the issue and not the people who brought the issue to my attention. I continued to build up my direct reports and focused on not diminishing their leadership. Soon, people started to believe communicating with me really had no ramifications.

Promoting engagement isn't about the employees trusting and respecting leadership; it's about leadership trusting employees. Employees of today are both intelligent and capable. They don't need your permission to do great work; they only need the tools to make it happen and a deep understanding of the why in the business. Your ability to make the mission real and believable and offering the support to get the job done is critical. A leader's role has gone from the controllers of the industrial age who made demands on their employees to today's facilitators and motivators who empower their employees. Get out of the way and spend your time creating an environment that is safe, respectful, collaborative, and transparent.

The move from hierarchy to a flat organizational structure requires a two-way trust system. Old school procedures need to be replaced with ingenuity, creativity, inventiveness, and solution-oriented thinking. The flat and trusting organization needs to back off the overwhelming number of metrics that can measure performance and focus on the metrics that matter. When employees feel 100 percent trusted, they're willing to stick their necks out and make a difference on the team and with customers.

Building new management muscle for what lies ahead is critical. Technology has gone from a budget or operating line item to an enabler of almost every strategy. As a leader, technology affects every part of the business and being completely fluent about how to use data and technology is a must.

Technology will affect your team. As work is reinvented, you must think about building the next generation of skills needed to drive the future and identify what is no longer needed. Some traditional career paths may disappear, but the need to develop people will be critical to retaining your high-potential people and creating a vision for those team members who come next. Understanding their interests and the needs of the business will allow to you to create the right path.

Lastly, a flat organizational structure will require you to rethink resources. Change is hard. People are hardwired toward the status quo and resist changing their assumptions and approaches even in the face of evidence. Allocating resources based on the past will drag on your performance. In fact, McKinsey reported that between 1990 and 2000, companies that made intentional decisions to allocate toward future needs drove a 30 percent higher return to their shareholders. The bar will continue to be raised in your future, rewarding those who can move with agility and speed.

Leaders and organizations may become frozen by the magnitude of the changes underway or may be unable to tackle them using outdated intuition. Taking a long view provides a better understanding of the depth, breadth, and the radical nature of the change, as well as the opportunities that will present themselves on the way.

One of the best books written on this topic is *Think Like a Futurist* by Cecily Sommers. She focuses the reader's attention on what is really changing, what isn't, and what's next. She gives practical approaches to breaking away from the "permanent present" and people's natural bias for projecting the past into the future. As soon as you understand the new framework of how things work together, you can find the long-term vision, see the opportunities, and lead the team with confidence.

# 23

# RETOOLING YOUR FEEDBACK LOOP

*A*s you're going up the ladder, seeking feedback from diverse networks is critical. Being intentional about this allows you to do the following:

1.  Retool your network feedback loop at every promotion to get a real, unbiased perspective.

2.  Enable more robust scenario planning. Making decisions should never be about the efficiency of the process; it should be about the effectiveness. Your ability as a leader to identify your natural biases is critical to allowing you to see the real facts.

As I moved up the ladder, I learned that being intentional about seeking feedback from diverse networks was critical to how I led an organization. Building your feedback loop and learning how to optimize you and your team is a lifelong journey. You can't go to any school or take any course; you learn it in real time through your careers, relationships, and activities. Only you can do the work. The process of debriefing, evaluating your experiences, using the framework, and utilizing that insight to sharpen your game are the disciplines that will allow you to move forward.

The move to an executive or C-suite position can make getting real feedback tough. I soon realized the feedback loops I had been using didn't work in the C-suite. Now everyone who showed up at my door wanted to sell me on what he or she thought was the next best thing for me to support. Even my presence in a meeting changed the dynamics and altered what people said.

I've learned the feedback I get often isn't the best information, because the people aren't sitting in my chair and don't have my viewpoint. I needed to develop the nose for finding the right sources and detecting distortion. Building diverse feedback loops to see multiple perspectives is one of my biggest learnings from the C-level.

Bottom line, I learned that people want my approval. Giving feedback and solid game-changing evaluations is in direct conflict. I got really good at being intentional about building a broad base of people willing to have candid conversations with me, so I could review key learnings and move forward with a new perspective. I learned to never rely on only one person's perspective. My job is to collect the feedback and connect the dots from those closest to me as well as those more distant. The broader and more diverse the group, the more I can cross-check what I'm hearing and be certain that I have the best feedback. I've become proficient at the art of asking questions, really listening, and understanding both what is said and what is left unsaid.

The environment in the C-suite can be so full of adversity—politics, siloed executive teams, inherited decisions—that it can undermine confidence and courage, which are key to being an effective leader. As a leader, you need to work hard to see the dynamics and norms of your new team so you don't assume them as your go forward. Establishing a dynamic and open feedback process is critical and fights against others in the executive ranks who want to be seen as the key player. The focus isn't on power, but rather the process you set up to drive the right behavior. Not focusing on this process will leave the norms as they are and will ultimately undermine what you're doing.

Some of the most important leadership competencies, now and in the future, are leading cross-functionally, leading transformation, and managing risk. The pace of the world makes it impossible to know everything. It requires a team of diverse understanding and skills to work together to make an impact. This issue is critical as the world gets more diverse and intertwined. To build and lead teams of increasing diversity requires transparent communication and the demonstration of empathy. If people know you facilitate open communication with all levels and appreciate people who are different than you, they'll be more open. The objective isn't about being part of your club; it's about having conversations that achieve and support the collective objectives. This more collaborative approach is a critical bridge as organizations find themselves in unfamiliar territory, tackling complex uncertainties about the economy, world stability, emerging technologies, cybersecurity, and more.

In the end, the C-suite is about showing up every day and jumping in the fire with your team with the conviction to do what is right. The C-suite requires both discipline and urgency in using a feedback-loop process to build a stronger base of self-awareness and a mindful center of confidence. The net result of doing both these things is a clear focus and optimization of your role in the C-suite.

# 24

# LEADING SO YOUR PEOPLE KNOW THEY MATTER

*T*he biggest issue I see from my chair is that leaders aren't focused on the impact of human nature and how human potential can be harnessed to build better companies and organizations. *Period.*

For most companies, 70 percent of operating expenses are in human capital. Let me be clear: If they aren't the right people, then that other 30 percent doesn't matter much. I would argue that even the economy doesn't matter—plenty of companies have thrived during tough times.

And the problem isn't technology or processes either. If I were to make a product, say coffee cups, I'd research the market and the equipment needed to make the cups. I'd look at my company's production capability/capacity, return on capital requirements, and distribution. Then, when I made the selection and secured working capital, I would set up production, train the people, and prepare to maintain the equipment. Then I'd go to the production people and say, "The equipment can do ten cups an hour. Can you figure out a way to improve the productivity to produce twelve an hour? And the response is usually a resounding yes! Your team loves to improve processes and results.

This isn't what leaders do with people. Leaders leave the human capital to chance, and doing so is a critical error. Human potential is one of the main reasons why I wrote this book.

Most companies continue to employ leaders who have proven that they don't maximize the human potential of their team members. In fact, they often do the opposite and get less from their people, not more. Can you imagine in my coffee cup example if I had started getting only eight or six or two cups per hour and were okay with the results? No, neither can I! But that's what leaders do with human capital. If you operated this way with your working capital, you would be out of business.

Then why do companies and organizations tolerate loss in human capital? The costs are enormous and put a drag on organization. The impact on a company or an organization performance is jaw dropping. In fact, Gallup has proven through their decades of research that when the same care is taken on the human potential side, it adds up to 59 percent growth in revenue per employee. Wow! Then why? Why? Why?

Because of leadership.

In the C-suite, people need to quit accepting excuses from others and themselves. Yes, managing people is hard, but that's a C-suite leader's job. Harnessing the human potential is the price of entry to be a leader at any level. This type of attitude has to start in the C-suite to have any chance to survive.

As a C-suite leader, selecting the right managers is one of the toughest jobs. Gallup reports that companies get it wrong 82 percent of the time. But companies can improve the odds if they change their criteria. The strategies aren't brain surgery, but they do require intense focus as a leader to ensure they take hold. The rewards are worth it, but they won't come overnight.

## Identifying Your Team's Strengths

Every leader starts with existing team members. Very few get to start from scratch. The focus on the team needs to be building self-awareness of your teams, one person at a time, to put them in a position to understand their unique strengths. You then need to develop them within the context of who they are, instead of making your people fit a standard version of what the role should be. When you help individuals optimize their skill set and personal motivation, the entire team will learn how to work together better, because they'll understand the power of the team's individual strengths.

I have used Gallup's StrengthsFinder tool in several organizations to successfully build collaborative teams. I especially like how the tool gives insight into dimensions. I also like the Hogan Development Survey, which is part of the Hogan Leadership Forecast series. Among other things, the results can give you a sense of what you look like at your worst or what is commonly referred to as your "dark side." Both of these tools were discussed earlier in the book in "Trying You On."

Additionally, in the C-suite you have to consider the metrics you use in evaluating your human capital. The metrics must be based on values that motivate your people to be in the business in the first place rather than the stock price or comparable store sales. The metrics must also reinforce the value of the mission and its impact, not just the financials.

Values are the results of people's efforts. Values force you to demonstrate the courage to work together and make it happen. You can never spend too much time bringing clarity to the goal, establishing the metrics from which progress will be measured, focusing together to drive a new behavior for desired results, and updating your plan as you get smarter together. Great things can emerge in challenging times when you lead and engage at all levels.

Unfortunately, I've lived in environments where it's common practice to focus on cutting costs without regard to whether it fractures the culture or drives value to the customers. It never ends well. The organizations lose momentum and begin a decline. Then, to make matters worse, some of those organizations change leadership as evidence of progress and call it a fresh start. I call it "rinse and repeat."

## Building Leaders

Your ability as a C-level leader to build leaders within the organization will be directly related to your ability to be clear about what matters to you. The C-level environments I have been in tested my self-awareness and my ability to build human capital. Specifically, I found I had to be clear about three things: where my passion and strengths meet with what my organization needs, where I add value, and lastly, where I have weaknesses or blind spots. Clarity about these three things allowed me to do my best work in the C-suite. If any of these are out of alignment, I know my ability to make progress in the C-suite is slim.

# 25

# UNDERSTANDING TONE AND THE DECISIONS AT THE SEAMS

As a C-suite leader, you need to understand the tone of your organization, both overall and in the different layers of the organization. You can have an enthusiastic layer next to you, but getting into your organization a bit deeper may not have the same tone because of the people or leader in the group. When you're at the top, getting a sense of where things are at is critical, because if the tone of the overall organization doesn't match that of smaller factions, you won't make progress and then won't understand why. Likewise, changing leadership takes time for the entire organization to feel the new tone—the new energy, direction, and thinking—so you must be intentional about identifying and sharing the new tone.

Over the course of my C-suite career, I've led in a variety of situations. Although I've worked in many positive situations, the organizations with the most negative tone brought the biggest life lessons. I've worked in hostile and dysfunctional environments where employees undermine each other and the organization. I've uncovered small employee factions who have banded together as a way to survive and endure. I've had bosses with egos and control issues that suffocated the talent in the organization. I've found scared employees who have been beaten down at every turn and lost their will to move forward. But in each case, I've also found employees who want to make a difference and who are excited to tackle new opportunities and improve their performance.

How do you discover the tone when you're accepting a new assignment? I've found it valuable to hold preliminary discussions with my team, on both a group and individual basis. Sometimes I would get pretty straightforward information about an organization's tone; other times I needed to read between the lines, especially when I didn't encounter a consistent tone throughout the organization. In larger group discussions, I'd uncover the accepted norms and theories of people in the organization, both of which help set the tone. In one-on-one conversations with current leaders, I'd often find the reason behind an organization's less-than-positive tone. I talked to leaders frustrated over their organization's lack of performance and to other leaders who had clearly lost the connection to the company's frontline issues. And over and over again, I'd find leaders who didn't even attempt to understand the issues affecting their organization and their people, so they couldn't solve the problems. I found leaders who chose to skim the surface and set expectations not grounded in reality and leaders who collected facts that matched their own reality and then complained about the gaps. Most important, I found that this type of C-level leadership doesn't make forward movement possible.

Let me share a simple example to illustrate the importance of understanding tone and also the importance of engaging your feedback loop to check the accuracy of your perception. During one of my monthly one-on-one meetings, I listened closely to an executive talk about his team. I heard frustration in his voice about how the directors and the young, high-potential employees didn't stay much past five o'clock, even in the heat of the battle.

I asked, "Was the work was getting done?"

He nodded, "Yes, but don't they want to do more?" In his mind, the tone of his team was "just enough, no more."

I asked him, "Have you asked them why they leave at five o'clock?"

He shook his head and said, "No."

The next month, the executive came back into my office shocked. He learned that his employees were paying late fees for every minute they were late in picking up their kids from daycare. Now, he understood that his employees' behavior wasn't driven by their lack of motivation, but rather by these fees. The simple step of seeking to understand the frontline issues is critical. It changed this executive's entire perception of the tone of his team.

## Decisions at the Seams

As a C-suite leader, you play a critical role in making sure decisions at the seams go smoothly. Decisions at the seams happen when more than one department or unit is responsible for making and implementing a decision. As the baton gets passed from one unit to another, the approaches might not quite match, especially if the units are operating in silos and don't have an overall picture. Team members can easily do their work and check the done box without any regard for the work that they need to do to connect their work to the next step. Leadership ensures that they do connect and that your people understand the entire context.

This is especially critical at times of transition. At one company, a change in consumer behavior caused buying dynamics to change, affecting the overall order count, the average sale, and the add-on sales. This meant that the unit of measure that had historically marked progress in the organization no longer told the entire story, requiring an entirely new metric based on the changing demands of the marketplace. When business models change, it requires new thinking and an evaluation of the entire system to ensure everything moves in alignment with the new direction. This is a classic example of how the decisions leaders are making in the C-suite impact every part of the organization and the many seams that connect them.

The C-suite's connection to the front line is vital in understanding tone and decision at the seams. Here's an example from my own career. I was thirty days into a new job, and I was traveling with the sales team. Sales were stagnant and had been for many years, which put the profit under pressure. The tone of the group was veering close to desperate and downtrodden.

But over the course of ten weeks of focused travel, we were able to develop a new go-to market approach that gave us a point of differentiation with our competition. We were able to increase sales because we used our traveling time and debriefs at dinner to replay the day and discuss ways to optimize our experience. The team's tone went from desperate to enthusiastic, and I was able to communicate back to the home office to make sure other departments were ready to do their part at the seams to handle this increase in sales.

Here's another example, this time from my time in a C-level retail sales role. We were having financial difficulties, so the company launched a new look to our product and a new way of business that challenged every part of how we used to do business. We moved from a compliance-driven culture to an employee-empowered focus, which had made the new look possible by empowering the employees to build a relationship with the consumer and tell their story in a unique way. The initial reaction was very positive, but when people started putting it into practice, it felt unfamiliar. And when the initial attempts didn't always hit the mark, people started to revert back to what they knew.

To recapture the enthusiasm for our new approach, I went on the road for nine weeks with a sales team. We held road rallies to allow the individual team members to share their work, celebrate forward movement, and offer suggestions to each other. The purpose wasn't to judge, but rather to encourage a collective commitment to help each other be better. I used questions similar to those used in the debrief sessions in the "Getting Past the Emotional" section. "What would you change to make this better? If you could do it again, what would you optimize to make it better?"

Slowly we saw progress. Then we published the results to show other employees what was possible. Publishing the results provided other teams a recipe for success, which translated into forward movement throughout our business, and ultimately, our entire industry. By understanding the complexity of the situation one piece at a time, we were able to see how each piece was stitched to the next to form a successful whole.

## UNDERSTANDING TONE AND THE DECISIONS AT THE SEAMS

Think about the feedback and observations as a big quilt. How things connect at the seams is vitally important to the health of an organization. This process didn't take lots of money. What it took was engagement, discipline, and time to make the difference. Leading with intention so that each individual, like each piece of a quilt fit together, is what made it all possible.

In other words, make it a priority to understand how the decisions at the seams of your organization come together. In the retail example, the previous compliance culture enforced policy and the rules. Empowering the people changed the focus to what could be improved, not what was wrong or didn't comply. The process provided context to the entire organization and enabled the C-level executives to connect the dots and be engaged, which is one of the most important parts of the job.

# 26

# LEADING INNOVATION AND CHANGE

*I* define *innovation* as the creativity to imagine new ideas and the courage to drive ideas in the face of adversity. The net result gives you new ways to do things that ultimately improve your life.

Innovation and change are hot topics in the business world. I have yet to meet an executive that, when asked, doesn't list innovation as a top priority. I see innovation and change in mission statements, in long-term strategies, and in budgets. When I look deeper, I also see innovation in system initiatives, in innovation councils, and in review of ideas. I even hear about innovation in conversations.

However, all of these different aspects of innovation ignore the most powerful component: the people who power innovation and change efforts. As a result, many innovation efforts never get off the ground and most never reach full potential.

The focus on people is imperative for the C-suite, especially the CEO, the leader of the organization. Innovation and change is personal; therefore, it starts with the C-level leader. The ability of a CEO to demonstrate a level of "fitness" and ability to innovate personally is critical. If the C-suite leaders aren't innovative from a personal perspective, the organization won't be able to make change happen.

I have seen it happen too many times. In schools, in organizations from very small to very large, in nonprofits, and in community service organizations—change affects everyone, including the leader. If the C-suite is unwilling to commit, there is no reason to waste the organization's time and resources, because the ending will be the same.

Even with a committed leader, the team can't go from zero to game ready without building the muscle, competency, and fitness level to make the change and innovation happen. Think of it another way: What if the CEO decided everyone in the organization was going to go skiing in the mountains, run a marathon, or hike a mountain trail? The CEO could buy all the latest gear and supplies for all the team members, and they would appear ready for the new adventure. But the new adventure will likely fail if the CEO and the team lack the ability to endure the activity.

C-suite leaders need to think differently about change and innovation. Their life experiences often shape their brains to favor the quick, direct connections needed to absorb knowledge. C-suite leaders overlook the meandering, associative networks innovation requires. Another barrier to innovation is that humans don't like change and prefer the comfort of things that look and feel the same. Lastly, humans are feeling animals that think, so igniting the passion of your people is critical. As a leader, igniting the passion is directly related to the ability to be clear about the why the change is needed and ensure that the why is grounded in empathy for those you serve.

To build a mind-set and culture of innovation, the CEO must be a learning leader, which means being vulnerable and practicing out loud with the team. A willingness to share mistakes and learn together doesn't weaken a CEO. It builds power and makes it possible for change to happen in real time because you're engaged and working alongside the team. By modeling the behaviors you seek while helping people accelerate their skills and abilities, you make it clear that innovation and the associated change is what is expected. Working alongside your team members enables them to demonstrate their courage and embrace the change, too.

In the C-suite, the pressure to deliver results can drive some C-level leaders to think they have to go big or go home. The notion that this approach demonstrates the courage and guts of a leader is nothing more than an ego trip. In reality, the ego trip drags down the organization and sucks the wind out of the teams charged with delivering the new initiatives.

Keeping the ego in check while remaining confident and advocating innovation and change is a tricky balance. C-level ego is something that can quickly kill the passion of the team and take away the very thing that allows the team to push through the head winds of leading innovation.

The trick for the C-level leader is to focus on the right things with the right people while keeping the scale manageable. The balance gives the organization the necessary room to learn and improve. At times, the process will be both messy and iterative, both for the C-suite and the organization as a whole. But the innovation and change process will speed up in the long run. When C-suite leaders let go of their egos and focus on people, the organization will be primed to experience the breakthrough, accidental discoveries, and unexpected outcomes that matter.

Lastly, C-suite executives should be using a process to evaluate ideas and innovations. Innovation is about doing, which sometimes means exploring an idea or concept to understand it better so you can go further. Without a strict process for evaluating innovation, the organization simply can't know whether the idea will work. The ability to take action is a key behavior for innovation where uncertainty is a given. Making decisions solely based on statistics and algorithms is sound when things are stable. C-level leaders must learn to balance the company's need for control, tracking, and resource management with the more minimal bureaucracy needed to foster innovation.

In the end, most innovations become failures unless the learning is applied in go-forward plans. Teaching the organization how to "do failure" on a small scale increases productivity and requires courage from the C-suite leadership to drive ideas forward in the face of adversity. When you as a leader give room to admit when things didn't work or failed, it removes some of the personal risk and allows people to engage more fully. Your people don't want to let you down. They want to get it right. But that isn't how life works. When they know you embrace the learning too, it opens up an entirely different environment and encourages people to be more open to trying things and less focused on perfect. Learning to frame innovation priorities in the context of the overall plan and understanding the organization's readiness for change is critical to success in the C-suite.

# 27

# CREATING YOUR EXECUTIVE PRESENCE

*I* found out quickly that advancing to the C-suite meant thinking about my executive presence at a whole new level. I had to focus on the way I looked, the words I used when I spoke, the way I carried myself, and the way I "showed up." People only know what they see. Learning to be conscious of your presence is critical. Sure, the quality of my work made a difference, but other tangible and intangible factors, including packaging, ego, and reputation, are also key differentiators in career advancement, especially if you're seeking an executive-level position.

**Your Packaging**

My executive presence or package is a direct reflection of who I am, which is one of the most important stories an executive share's with employees, coworkers, and clients. The executive package helps tell the story of who you are and why. The most important aspect of building the executive package is authenticity. For example, some executives can pull off jeans and cowboy boots and leather because the style fits the organization's tone and culture and is also authentically who they are. For others, dressing this way looks forced or makes people want to ask if they're going to a costume party, because it just doesn't fit.

The executive package is made up of three key components. According to a study by the Center for Talent Innovation, a combination of grace under fire, dignity, presence, influence, emotional intelligence, reputation/credibility, and vision accounts for 62 percent of your package. Communication skills make up 31 percent and include speaking ability, ability to command a room and read an audience, use of assertiveness, use of humor, and use of posture and body language. The remaining 7 percent is how you look with the biggest element being grooming. Do you look polished and pulled together? Are you current and up to date? Seven percent may seem like a small number to worry about, but I've seen cases where people didn't get the nod because their style didn't properly reflect what the organization was looking for.

With physical presence, I have some natural advantages. I am fortunate to be five-ten—taller than most women. My height gives me a physical advantage in the way I show up, because whether it's fair or not, most people automatically perceive taller people as having more authority.

Some of my other packaging didn't come as naturally, such as my wardrobe. Because I'm not a huge shopper, I had to prioritize finding clothing that suited the tone of the organizations and my C-level role. I wanted a sense of style without the extra time, so I focused on finding wardrobe pieces that would last and were timeless. For me, working with a trusted salesperson in my favorite clothing stores was the key. Over the course of my career, I have worked with three primary people who understand my style and me. Their goal is to optimize me and push me a bit, but not try to make me into someone I'm not, despite what's in fashion that year. If the C-suite is your goal, find a person or team who can help guide your clothing choices, even if you think you're good at finding what works for you. Their perspective can help add an extra touch that finishes your look.

**Your Ego**

Combating ego involves staying healthy, both physically and mentally. The ego demands in the C-suite are real. For me, I've never kept score by comparing myself against what others have or do. I've always focused on my impact on others. In fact, over the years, watching some executives get all puffed up to demonstrate their power has become a source of humor for me. It looks foolish and diminishes the impact of their leadership. Don't forget that all leaders put their shirts on the same way.

Early in my career, a wise executive shared advice about ego. He said, "You will be successful beyond your wildest dreams. Learn early how to keep your ego in check. If you don't, it is only a matter of time before it gets the best of you." So I take time to remember my roots, spend time at the cabin, take a walk with my husband, eat dinner as a family, do my yard work and household chores, and spend time with friends—these experiences give my ego the perspective I need. Doing some of these simple tasks and prioritizing the people I care about are great ways to keep your ego in check.

**Your Reputation**

Reputation, for me, is earning the distinction that I left an organization a better place than when I arrived. Too many times, I see leaders hang on past their time. Many times, the next part of an organization's history needs a different leader to take it to the next level. The best way to kill a reputation is by not leaving when it's time to leave.

> *"Someone's sitting in the shade today because someone planted a tree a long time ago."*
>
> —*Warren Buffet*

Today more than ever, building a reputation in the C-suite means demonstrating the ability to bridge the gap between the collective wisdom of the older employees and the innovative ideas of the new regime. It will show your commitment to not discriminate. Only when every generation and discipline is willing to be open and learn lessons from the other will you as a leader be able to truly maximize the potential of your organization.

In this connected world, understand that everything you do—your track record and feedback about who you are and what you do—is visible and will be shared. It's like living in a small town, except today, you—and everyone else—are just a click away from seeing the real picture, so take extra care because reputations take years to build, but moments to unravel if left unattended.

# SECTION V: LEADING FROM THE BOARDROOM

**Expanding Your Leadership Reach . . .**

This section is short. It's designed to give you a brief perspective of leadership from the boardroom. I hear a lot of people talk about their desire to serve on a board, but I find most don't really understand what it entails. Serving on a board is a prestigious thing to talk about. However, board leadership shouldn't be about building individual importance; it should be about using your experience to help another organization be successful.

# 28

## KNOWING WHEN YOU'RE READY

Whether you serve on a nonprofit, community, or corporate board, the role of a board member is a serious one that requires leadership different from anything else you've experienced. You're leveraging your leadership experience to benefit another organization. Being on the board isn't about the status; it's about leading so the organizations you serve can have a bigger impact.

Before I had my boys, I earned my MBA at the University of St. Thomas in St. Paul, Minnesota. I was only about thirty years old, but I knew after talking to many leaders that I wanted to be on a board of directors someday. It seemed like a logical step in my leadership journey, but I must admit, I didn't understand the role any better than most.

My Executive Perspectives class is where I gained better insight on board leadership from both my professor and guest speakers. This was the first time I interacted personally with people who served on boards. My professor served on several prominent boards and was recognized by the community as a top board director.

I spoke to him several times after class about his experiences, and he inspired me to learn more. I was four months pregnant when I graduated, and he knew building a family was a priority for me. I remember telling him, "Let's stay in touch, and when I'm ready to explore a board role more seriously, I'd like to connect with you." He said, "I'd love to have the conversation with you when you're ready, Nancy."

Seven years later, after having two boys and assuming greater leadership roles at work, I felt ready. I called my professor and asked him to meet me for lunch. We met in the university cafeteria. After updating each other, I reminded him about our conversation on board service. Much to my surprise, he remembered. I shared my current thinking with him.

"Tom, the Executive Perspectives class was one of my best classes," I said. "You inspired me to think bigger, and I've been interested in corporate board work ever since. Now I think I'm ready to learn more about the role and how to get started. I was hoping to pick your brain to help me figure out where to begin."

He sat back, and after what seemed like a long pause, he looked at me and asked, "How old are you?"

"Thirty-eight," I said.

"How about your boys?" he asked.

"Erik is eight and Jorgen is four," I answered.

Again, the pause seemed to last forever.

"Nancy, spend time with your family. Join the PTA and get involved with organizations that serve your kids," Tom said. "Your time to serve on a board of directors will come, but right now, your time is better spent with your kids, swinging at the park and sitting at the dinner table."

Tom's advice wasn't really what I wanted to hear. In fact, I was initially offended and a little taken aback since his response didn't fit my pre-determined plan. But I respected his candor, and intuitively, I knew he was right. His wealth of knowledge and experience allowed him to be a student of the situation/person/issue and provide the right perspective to help gain a new perspective.

## Researching Board Opportunities

About five years later, when Jorgen was in middle school and Erik had just started high school, I started to do some preliminary research on organizations that would be a good fit for my expertise. Tom had suggested starting with nonprofit boards so I began exploring options, focusing first on organizations where I had a personal connection with the organization and its mission. I was pleased to be invited to join the board of trustees at my undergraduate alma mater, Gustavus Adolphus College. It was a great opportunity to contribute and to learn about board service.

Five years later, while exploring opportunities to share my business expertise, a friend recommended I look into the Bloomington Chamber of Commerce. I was interested in the intersection of business, community, and government. The complexity of issues facing society today would be front and center on this board, and it focused on the community where I both lived and worked. I joined that board, and later, the YMCA, an organization important to my entire family.

I also thought about other organizations that had impacted me where I could now give back. After some thought, Family, Career, and Community Leaders of America (FCCLA) rose above all the others. In high school, I was a state officer of the organization, then known as Future Homemakers of America. My experience had a profound effect on my leadership and still shapes how I work today.

I found the national website for the FCCLA and sent a note offering my help. I initially didn't hear back from anyone. About a month later, the media director at FCCLA reached back and wanted to write a bio on me. I was honored to be featured in the organization's publication as a role model, but I told him I was interested in doing more. He helped connect me with the Minnesota state office. Eventually, I reached the executive director, and we met to explore how my skills and talents aligned with the needs of the organization. Within twenty-four hours, she sent me her top ten ideas for how I could help. One conversation led to another, and soon, I was sitting on the board of directors for the Minnesota chapter of the FCCLA.

## Finding the Right Board for You

Now that I've been on several boards, I have developed a process to determine if a board is a good fit for me. Although some of this information relates only to corporate boards, the key point—knowing the organization, its management, and its board thoroughly—is germane to all boards that you're considering.

Most importantly, you need to understand the challenges that the board is facing. I take extra time to inquire and do due diligence on the strategic plan, market dynamics, risks/opportunities, the current management's effectiveness (CEO, management team, and CFO), quality of board members and their collective portfolio of skills, the relationships of board members to each other and management, and board expectations on the frequency of meetings and committee involvement.

My process includes interviews of board and management leadership, as well as conversations with key contacts outside of the organization. The interviews show me the behaviors, trends, and focus of the board over a longer time frame. I also conduct a review of historical documents, including the last two years of board minutes. The board minutes reveal valuable data on how the information is presented and processed, the attendance of board members, and how decisions are really made. This review allows me to discern who the key influencers are and whether a herd or groupthink mentality exists.

The interviews and board minutes additionally give me an idea of the organization's capacity for flexibility and change. An ability to change with the times is the one capacity that allows companies to last a hundred years or longer. If the board is made up of too many generalists or people who lack current experience, it significantly lengthens the time required to convince them to move forward, and these board members won't push management hard enough to see what lies ahead. In these situations, opportunities will be missed, and the real impact of the important decisions will get lost.

In other cases, I've seen board members who are too quick to change a credible corporate strategy because of intense market pressure. The board members change their minds, but refuse to provide additional support for more focus in this area. I've seen this happen when the board fell victim to the timing of quarterly and annual deadlines versus doing the work to understand what forward progress should look like and under what time frame they should see results.

Before I take a board member role, I make it a priority to know who is on the board. I take the time to understand the individual and the collective makeup of the board to see how I fit. I investigate their individual track records and the overall ability of the board to influence outcomes and engage in functional board activities. I ask myself if I can work with this group in good times and in bad. I've learned to be thoughtful and comprehensive to fully vet the situation.

I remember the first time I was approached to serve on a board. Trust me, being asked to be a board member is extremely flattering. It's easy to bask in the accolades, and I still do, but only for a few moments, by expressing my gratitude for their offer. But now I quickly move on to digging deeper. Why do the board members want me? What do they think I can contribute? How do they think I will make a difference and provide valuable insight? What are the skills, expertise, and experience specifically that they value from me? How do I fit into their current slate of board members and what do they think they will need in the future?

I pay careful attention to the evolution of the board quality and caliber. Am I helping the board keep the status quo or am I bringing something new that is needed for the future? What are the expectations for my board service—committees, time commitments, and frequency? What are the travel requirements between meetings? Are there any conflict of interest guidelines I need to understand?

Remember: board service is an important role. A lot of diligence is necessary to vet out the opportunity. Take the time to educate yourself by talking to other board members or board associations to help you gain a fuller context of the board evaluation process.

# 29

# UNDERSTANDING THE BOARD MEMBER ROLE

*A*t the age of thirty, after finishing my MBA, I didn't fully understand the board member role. Even in my first board member role twelve years later, I didn't completely comprehend the impact of the board members on the organizations that they serve. Although I now feel well versed, my understanding of the boardroom and the impact of the board member role are constantly evolving as I gain new experiences from my different vantage points in each boardroom.

You can easily underestimate the level of preparation and engagement required to be a high-impact board director. You can't rely on your past experience. Your engagement requires an intentional effort to have the appropriate engagement and perspective to impact the decisions made in the boardroom. I currently sit on four boards, including both nonprofit and corporate boards. In addition, I've made it a priority to improve my board understanding by completing the National Association of Corporate Directors (NACD) Board Leadership Fellow credential.

The first time I sat at the boardroom table, I looked across at the other members and wondered how I would fit in and what expertise I would become known for. Now, at age fifty-three with my experience on nonprofit and corporate boards, I have a broader base of experience and expertise to bring into the boardroom. I recently went to a national board member conference sponsored by NACD where 1,500 board members from all over the country gathered. A young man in his thirties spoke about technology and cybersecurity and the expertise gap that exists between the young professional and the typical board member who is much older.

Someone asked him, "Do you think we need to have younger board members with this type of cybersecurity expertise sitting on our boards?"

He responded, "No. As board members, you have to be aware of the impact of technology, but it's more important to have years of experience in corporations, while remaining committed to being a student of emerging issues. The younger professional may have the technical expertise but not the knowledge of running a large corporation."

I found that to be an insightful comment because I believe the only way to understand the boardroom is through direct, in-the-field experience in C-level roles, together with a thirst for being a student of the marketplace. One without the other is a journey to irrelevance in the boardroom.

After my experiences sitting on boards, I now believe having expertise and experience is what understanding the boardroom and the board member role takes. This is exactly why, almost twenty years ago, my professor advised me to wait before pursuing a board position. The experience gave me the perspective to engage and add value.

Today, most people would say that boards aren't working. More than a decade has passed since Enron and the many changes in regulatory reform that resulted, yet the stats say that boards are still falling short of their core mission: providing strong oversight and strategic support for management's efforts to create long-term value.

In fact, a McKinsey report indicated that only 34 percent of board members fully comprehend their company's strategies, only 22 percent were completely aware of how their firms created value, and only 16 percent claimed that their boards had a strong understanding of the dynamics of their firm's industry. Evidence also suggests that boards are the ones who push for short-term financial results and underemphasize long-term value creation. Overall, the boards cite themselves 47 percent of the time and with public companies that statistic escalates to 74 percent.

In contrast, boards that combine deep relevant experience and build knowledge independent of the company can drive different results. The independent board pushes companies from their business-as-usual practices to be more intentional about where they invest their resources. The effective and high-functioning board kicks the company out of low gear and drives a resource reallocation to meet the future. McKinsey research over a twenty-year period showed that when capital was strategically shifted, the organizations delivered a 30 percent higher return to shareholders.

A board's job is to help the company see around the corner. The job requires board members to bring their real-life experiences, be a student of the business, and shed light on possible scenarios. The three most common issues I have witnessed in the board room are the following: board members who rely on their past experience too much and push it forward to today; board members who act and behave as if they're still management; and board members who don't dig deep enough into the details or the risks to be effective. As a result, discussions stay at the 150,000-foot level and lack perspective from the ground floor where execution of the strategy happens.

Being a good board member requires real-world operating experience to truly understand the complexity and the inherent surprises that will surface in every plan, and therefore, the need for management to be agile and proactive in taking action. I have seen the effect of groupthink that diminished the critical thinking and resulted in bad results.

The best board members are great listeners and great questioners. When board members haven't listened or questioned or engaged in intense debates about the real company issues, they've failed to make a significant impact. The best board members understand what deserves their attention and don't let one-time occurrences to easily distract them. The net result of this type of intentional leadership in the boardroom: risk is reduced and opportunities surface.

# 30

# TRANSITIONING TO A BOARD MEMBER ROLE

*I*n this chapter, I will share some more specific insights I learned as a board member, including my understanding of the board member role for both nonprofits and corporate boards. I'll also talk about how to transition from a management to a board role and how to engage as a board member to have maximum impact.

As I mentioned in a previous chapter, you need to do additional research to understand the risks of board leadership, the differences between private versus nonprofit versus public boards, compensation, and other issues that I won't talk about here. I am a member of NACD, which I mentioned in the last chapter, along with the Women Corporate Directors (WCD) Foundation (www.womencorporatedirectors.com) and the Association of Governing Boards of Universities and Colleges (AGB) (www.agb.org). All three offer tremendous resources to learn more about the entire experience of serving on a board as well as professional development certification programs. I encourage anyone considering or currently working in a board role to explore these organizations and the education and support they offer.

The first step in any successful board transition is the orientation. Most of the time, the organization, whether nonprofit or for-profit, has an onboarding process for its board members. For me, the formal orientation process is the jump-start. After that, advocate for what you need to build your own orientation plan.

## Five Key Areas for Board Orientation

From my perspective, you need to know about five key areas for both the orientation and the ongoing board work. These are focused more on a corporate versus nonprofit situation, but most areas are germane to all organizations:

**Customer experience:** Every organization has a customer experience that drives its revenue and profit. Take time to engage with the organization as a customer would. Doing so allows you to take stock of the strategic implications of the marketing environment and the company's position with the customers. Seeing this firsthand can help you understand what earns revenue and what costs money. Understanding changes in customer habits will help you see the business model changes that are coming so you can be more proactive and engaged.

- **Follow the money:** How does the organization make money/generate revenue? What are the sources and uses of cash? How much of it really adds value? What are the risks? What are the trends of both revenue and expenses?

- **Marketplace dynamics:** The strategic plan is based on industry assumptions. These need to be clearly articulated so you can begin to understand the structure and economics on which the plan is built. Most boards spend most of their strategic time reviewing plans and just approving them, complete with management's bias. It leaves too much value on the table and makes the board vulnerable to surprises.

  When armed with a review of the marketplace fundamentals and a clear understanding of both the industry and company economics, boards are in a better position to have the kinds of informed discussion and debate with senior leadership that lead to better, smarter decisions. It also allows the strategic options and scenarios to be identified and vetted, which puts the team of management and the board in a better position to broaden the thinking and consider new, even unexpected outcomes. When the unexpected shows up, this work becomes the backdrop that drives more agility and nimbleness to make decisions with confidence.

- **Infrastructure:** With any scenario there is the question of how to allocate resources: people, capital, and other resources. A board or senior management can easily overlook how difficult it is to reconcile sweeping changes with the day-to-day operational realities. Extending the conversation to give visibility to the execution of change efforts is important. The conversation allows everyone to move at the same pace and with a common understanding come along with what is happening in the business.

- **Transparency** and visibility of the results also puts pressure on management to do its homework. This process puts a spotlight on the strategies and allows for the clearer alignment necessary to make bold moves. This in turn will build confidence in the decisions by both the board and the management team to commit resources needed for key change efforts. The conversation highlights possible issues—for example, where the training is hodgepodge or inadequate, the software systems substandard, or the operating processes are out of alignment with creating value for the customer.

- **People:** Remember my discussion about the importance of having the right structure, with the right people in the right chair? The ability of an organization to deliver on its promise and value to the customer and the shareholders/stakeholders is directly related to how well it selects, develops, and manages its human capital.

People, or human capital, typically represent 70 percent of the operating costs. Therefore, the board needs focus on human capital to understand and discuss the key dimensions of the human capital, including the most traditional, such as the key leaders and the high potentials. But the conversation needs to go deeper to more fully see how the leadership team is doing at developing and optimizing its human talent. Find out where the future talent is coming from and who is making that happen, as well as who is experiencing turnover or people issues. Too many times, this dimension isn't visible at the board level. You merely see the results measured in the financial statements.

Studies show that 70 percent of the variance in employee engagement is due to managers. Companies miss the mark on high managerial talent in 82 percent of their hiring decisions. However, when they get it right, it drives a 48 percent higher profit. When the number of talented managers increases and the rate of employee engagement doubles, companies achieve 147 percent higher earnings per share when compared to their competitors.

Taking time to truly vet this issue will put the board in a position to hold management's feet to the fire by using talent and leadership development as a key marker of success. Developing a view toward future talent demands— and how the organization will meet those demands— is critical and must include how the current structure is helping or hurting progress.

These five key areas are vital to using your board leadership to recognize and respond to changing environments, understand the customer experience, identify infrastructure that is not customer-centric and/or is too costly, ensure attention to the human capital, and demand clear accountability to drive results.

# TRANSITIONING TO A BOARD MEMBER ROLE

## Learning through Experience

Here I share some of my earlier board experiences to give you more insight on transitioning and contributing to a board. Successfully transitioning to a board member role isn't always easy. Several of my early board roles were challenging to figure out. The boards were just developing and so was I. Learning to understand how to provide the guidance needed by the management team to help the organization move forward was very different from running an organization. (See the previous chapter for more details about this.)

Working with other board members whom I didn't see often brought more challenges, which required spending time with them outside the board meetings. In fact, the time spent at the board meetings was minimal compared to the extra time it took to do the prep work, spend time with the people, learn the business, and gain perspective—which is essential if you want to be a strong contributor. I eventually learned which of my leadership skills were most transferrable to a board role, including the power of asking good questions and leveraging my experience to help company leadership see what may be ahead. These were great learning experiences for me, and, I hope, the rest of the board and the organizations themselves.

Later, I had an opportunity to work with a more established and larger board and management team. I had shared with several friends that I was looking for a board role in a larger nonprofit. One of them asked about my interest in an organization where she served on the governance committee. I had heard of the organization, but I really didn't know much about them.

A while later, the nonprofit's executive director was a keynote speaker at an awards ceremony where I was honored. She was impressive. I knew that one of her goals was to build a strong board that would strengthen the organization and could be a source of future board leaders for other organizations. I expressed my interest in joining the board.

Part of the nomination process was to have lunch with the executive director, the board chair, and the nominating committee. I wanted to ensure that the organization was one I could support, that the board members were engaged and not just building their resumes, and that the leadership was sound. Instantly, the executive director and I made a connection. We shared some of the same perspectives on leadership in the boardroom and how leadership and tone filters down to directly impact the organization. The executive director's ideas on having a broader perspective on her board of directors significantly impacted the way I operate as a board member to this day.

I was invited to join the board, where I learned two important lessons about the role of board member. The first lesson is "nose in, but fingers out." What does that mean? Well, management's job is to have "fingers in"—and run the business on a daily basis. As a board member, you keep your "nose in," to have a bead on what's going on, but you keep your fingers out of implementation. Some of the earlier nonprofit boards I worked with were working boards, meaning you were expected to take a more hands-on approach. Joining more mature nonprofit boards and corporate boards requires a different approach.

The second lesson is the importance of external thinking to help sharpen management's internal perspective. As a board member you can bring clarity and insight that isn't affected by the day-to-day struggles faced by management. A board member's job is to bring a fresh perspective, be thought provoking, and inspire the organization's senior leaders to do a better job and think more clearly in times of struggle. The board can also help ensure that there's clarity about the overall mission and goals, which allows the teams within the organization to do their best work.

Like any other leadership role, you need to be intentional about board leadership. The role is too important to not be thoughtful about how you'll impact an organization. Don't take a board position because you assume that it's the next step on your leadership journey. You should only consider becoming a board member because you feel ready and able to provide the right leadership and are willing to do the hard work to accomplish the job.

Ultimately, the board of directors can set the tone that drives the senior leadership and organization, both good and bad. For both the organization, and you as a board member, seeking a board that has a diverse range of thoughts but supports the overall mission of the organization is key to a successful experience.

# 31

# BEING A HIGH-IMPACT DIRECTOR

The board is ultimately responsible for setting the standards and strategic expectations of an organization, but often the board members find themselves too far removed from reality. I've seen board members who devote so much time reviewing numbers that they forget to spend time with the customers, influencers, and stakeholders. Boards must be both vigilant and willing to demand change in how management engages them and what opportunities are provided to learn and stay current about the organizations they serve.

More importantly board members must do their own homework from an independent viewpoint. Much of the information that board members receive comes from internal sources, particularly management. But looking for information from outside sources is also important. These outside sources give a broader context and perspective and allow the board members to see where the organization might be biased or misguided. When the board of directors has members who are all doing their jobs, then the proper strategic focus, governance, fiduciary, and risk oversight is in place.

Additionally, the board may need to push management to act with urgency. As a board member, I've found it most challenging when a long-time executive leadership exists, but the once-stable industry is now changing. To optimize results, forcing timely decisions by management is a critical skill in the repertoire of the adept board member.

Finally, demonstrating courage is a vital skill in the boardroom. As a board member, you must be willing to ask the questions even when others don't agree, support decisions even when everything isn't clear, and debate issues to ensure you understand them fully and that management has been thoughtful about alternatives.

The manner in which you address these issues is equally important. The tone you set can be tough and direct, but it should be in the spirit of helping the team win. The boardroom isn't a place to showcase your ego or to demonstrate how smart you are, only to diminish and belittle management. Your role is to ensure the future health and vitality of the organization by working with organizational leadership to get results.

The last trademark of being a successful, influential board member is the ability to authentically celebrate forward movement for the organizations and the individuals that drove the results. Too often, looking only at what needs attention fills all the board's time. I've found better results when the board takes a step back to acknowledge accomplishments and show how the organization is moving the ball down the field—even when all the milestones weren't reached. The ball moved down the field because the organization did the work. The recognition needs to be acknowledged. Sharing a positive outlook will energize the team and build momentum to continue the fight, even when it may be against all odds.

# SECTION VI: SHARING MY TOP TEN LIFE LESSONS

**My Insights so that You Can Have a Running Start . . .**

In the following chapters, I have captured my top ten life lessons. These chapters are also a summary of some of the book's key points, so you can turn to them again and again when you feel the need for a short refresher course. As with the rest of the book, my purpose is to jump-start your ability to optimize you. If my life's experiences can help you gain new insight, it has been worth my time to write and yours to read.

I know I have benefited from so many who have taken the time to share their journey with me. I have learned something each time. So this final section is dedicated to my top ten life lessons. I know there will be more as I keep learning and growing, because there were so many already that it was tough to decide which to share.

I chose these ten because they're vital to equipping you with a better approach to meeting the demands of leadership, both personally and professionally. In each case, I spend time taking about the *process* versus the *answer*. Learning how to live and lead your life with intention will build confidence that you can figure it out yourself.

In the end, being grounded in who you are allows you to be both nimble and disciplined in your approach to life. I hope this perspective gives you new insight and accelerates your ability to be your best every day.

# LESSON 1

# ALWAYS START WITH THE BIG PICTURE

*I*n leadership and in life, it's always best to start with the big picture. Doing so helps you understand how, what, and why you're doing what you're doing. Some people will argue, "I am the detail person, not the big picture person." Although some people have a preference for how they accomplish and think about their work, it's in your best interest to always start with a view of the whole and not just its parts.

When you look at the big picture first, it allows you to share a common mission and more fully understand the significance in the work before you put your head down and get to work. Then when you look up to reflect on how things are going, the conversation will be rich with ideas for alternate strategies, people will ask the important, high-level questions, and the result will bring focus, clarity, and ownership by the team.

Real leadership isn't just about seeing the big picture, but also about making sure others see it too, so that together you can create a shared vision. Leadership will inspire your team members to add value and their personal passion to the picture.

The stonecutters' story, which has been around in various versions for years, is a good illustration. I like the version told by Senge, in which the stonecutters were building St. Paul's Cathedral, designed by renowned British architect and designer, Sir Christopher Wren:

One day, after work on his cathedral had begun, Wren, unrecognized by the workforce, walked among the artisans and stonecutters.

He asked one of the workmen: "What are you doing?"

"I am cutting a piece of stone," the workman replied.

He asked the same question of the second stonecutter.

"I am earning five shillings two pence a day," the second workman replied.

He asked a third workman the same question, and the man answered, "I am helping Sir Christopher Wren build a magnificent cathedral to the glory of God."

The story does a wonderful job of showing the personal passion that can result when someone understands the big picture, which is one of the most important roles of leaders—to ensure that frontline workers understand their role in reaching the overall organizational role. It helps unleash their passions and be more engaged because they understand how their work accomplishes the bigger goal.

To look at a modern-day version of this concept and apply it to your life's work, here is a Facebook entry from one of my son's friends. He talks about the concept of big-picture thinking and his educational training:

"I graduate on Saturday and it's got me thinking reflectively on my time here at SDSU. Leaving high school, I remember hearing speeches about, 'exploring the next part of your life,' and, 'asking the big questions.' When I got to college, I heard speeches telling me to 'ask the big questions,' and when I graduate on Saturday I'm sure I will hear more speeches about "asking the big questions.' Here's the deal, we have been told to 'ask the big questions' for four years. In between all these speeches, we spend four years taking courses that train us to ask the little questions. We take specialized courses, taught by specialized professors, aimed at specialized students. What we receive on Saturday is a vocational training certificate that shows companies that we have the technical knowledge for the job."

I love his mom's response:

## ALWAYS START WITH THE BIG PICTURE

"The big questions in life have nothing to do with schooling, son. Seeking, and gaining, knowledge is an admirable thing. And you are very good at it, but the most important things in your life will always deal with faith, family, and friends. Having these things in your life will always bring you joy—and heartache. I think this is where the questions come from. Then you spend much of your life finding the answers. And remember, those guys are just trying to write a good speech. So proud of you!"

Whether in work or in life, the big picture is simply the entirety of what you're doing—your ultimate goal and how it relates to everything around you. You might think about it as an aerial view of your life. It shouldn't diminish the importance of the details that will take you from here to there. However, in order to get an accurate picture of where you are and where you're going, you need to step back periodically and take a high-level look. Doing so forces you to put value on the questions you've already asked and sparks your curiosity to explore and look at the situations differently. Practice a do-think-do rhythm as you try things on, reflect on them to understand them better, and then do something with this new understanding. There are no tests—just doing, reflecting, and then doing some more to figure it out. The more you practice this skill, the more robust you'll be at understanding how what you're doing today links with the significance of your life's work.

The processes that I've talked about in this book are the exercises I found help me learn and build this skill. This knowledge allowed me to override my natural tendencies where needed, and I encourage you to do the same thing.

## LESSON 2

# WHAT PEOPLE SEE IS WHAT PEOPLE THINK (ABOUT YOU)

*H*ow do you show up? You may be surprised. I know I was. I was three months into a new assignment and was meeting with a trusted mentor to check in. I cherished the time because I knew spending time together would help me gain a new perspective. The meeting started as it usually did with time to catch up on our lives and our families and share our perspectives on the world and our role in it.

We moved on to talk about my career. He was authentically curious about my new role and how it was going. We debriefed on the reality of the business and then moved to the critical changes that were needed. His insights helped me better see the big picture, both what brought us there and what could be.

Then we moved on to my role as a leader. He was excited about my new opportunity and the match to my skills. But, he said, "I can see the scope of this job is going to challenge you, as it would anyone." It was a new role, and no one had ever been asked to tackle it in this way. He knew I could do it, but he wanted to make sure I didn't miss anything. He asked me if I understood how I "show up."

I asked him to share more. "There is no doubt that you're busy, and you need to be, to do your job, but you look busy too," he said. "You need to change that if you really want to optimize what is possible, like I know you can."

Hmmmm, am busy, look busy. I don't understand.

"One of your gifts, Nancy, is your ability to listen, hear the voice of others, and be a student of the business," he continued. "Then you take your insights and craft a plan that builds an amazing future and takes everyone to a new place. People get behind it because they had a part of it, and your leadership helps them see how to optimize it. You need to continue to do that, but you need to remain approachable."

I pushed back and indicated that I had an open-door policy and that everyone knew how to get in touch. To which he replied, "But that doesn't mean they will. You need to make it easier."

I paused to try to understand. "Usually I'm a quick study, but there must be something I am missing," I said.

He smiled and shared more detail about how I show up. "I love how you engage with your people," he said. "But you're scheduled so tight, as soon as one thing is done, you're off to the next thing. Your pace doesn't allow you to take advantage of the in between times, and you're going to miss things. Some of the best insights come from lingering after the meeting to ponder the issues further. If you aren't present, your team members won't bring their thoughts to you. You have to be in the moment to hear the discussion."

We dug deeper. He asked me to be aware of how I walk. Really, I thought. Why does that matter? He said, "You're tall. You can walk faster than most, which gives the impression that you're in a hurry and not available."

"But I always say hi to everyone and engage in conversation," I said.

He agreed, but he told me that people were reluctant to stop me to engage. "You need to slow down so that you're approachable for hallway conversations, not just the greetings and friendly banter."

Again, I paused and reflected. He was right. I needed to make changes that would allow me to show up differently. I was missing opportunities because I was going too fast and missed some of the details that could make a difference.

So, during my next weekly meeting with my administrative assistant, we talked about the I'm-too-busy-to-talk message I was giving out and discussed what alterations we needed to make to my calendar to allow me to show up differently. In particular, we were more intentional about thinking about the purpose of each meeting so we could anticipate which in between times were most important. A few minor tweaks to my calendar scheduled open time between certain meetings, making a huge difference.

Changes take time. Slowing down allowed me to see the signs that things were going well—or not. Slowing down allowed me to engage more pro-actively with the teams to push things along or celebrate the forward movement so we could focus on the next steps and gain momentum.

Slowing down also allowed me to more proactively anticipate when I needed to plan a break in the action so I could recharge, and I made sure to let my team know well in advance when I would be gone. When people know your calendar, they'll plan around it to meet their responsibilities.

Role modeling a healthy approach shows your team how to take a break, too, which is important. Research shows that marathon hours and no downtime do more ill than good. The risk of heart disease increases 67 percent for workers that put in eleven hours a day versus eight, they're also three times more likely to develop an alcohol abuse problem if they work fifty+ hours a week, and their overall productivity will actually decline and their judgment will be impaired due to higher stress levels and less sleep.

This new approach also helped me plan my time differently. I could anticipate when I needed to block my time to get in the zone of what-ever was ahead of me and when I was open for interruption. Otherwise,

I handled well-intentioned interruptions in a reactive mode that robbed me of the time I needed to think more deeply about the business. I could only work in the business versus on the business. Working in the business can consume you in all the details. Working on the business allows you to have a boarder perspective and sometimes change the details to align to a new future.

Think about planning your unstructured time to be alone and to think deeply about the business. Unstructured time is the root source of ideas and connections between ideas and gives you time to see your way forward through complex problems and work toward solutions that were otherwise elusive.

Learn to manage your pace and understand how you really show up. The details do matter. Here is what I had to watch for: walking quickly in the hallways, using handwriting that appears to be written in hurry, scheduling my calendar, skipping lunch and therefore time to chat with employees in the lunchroom, planning time to be available when field people were in the office, being present in the hallways at annual meetings to chat with people, the time I arrived and left the office each day, canceling meetings, or arriving late on a regular basis. You simply won't see the signs if you're moving too fast. Managing your pace will also help you show up as your best you and allow you to serve yourself and your organization even better.

# LESSON 3

# LIVE (AND LEARN) WITH INTENTION

*A*chieving mastery status at anything requires relentless self-discipline, which also includes leading your life with intention. You must practice it endlessly, over and over again, with each practice session focused on getting better, just as a music lesson or sports workout is designed to do.

> *"You cannot build a dream on a foundation of sand. To weather the test of storms, it must be cemented in the heart with uncompromising conviction."*
>
> —*T.F. Hodges*

I've found that working on what I call the "The Magic Five"—time, focus, boundaries, debriefing, and curiosity—helps me improve my skill at living with intention.

## Time

I've talked several times in this book about the importance of using your time wisely. Doing so is the ultimate equalizer. Regardless of a person's stature in life, everyone gets the same amount of time every day, no matter how the person used it yesterday. Building your muscle, in time management, in other words, developing this skill, is important. If you don't, you will lose the opportunity to optimize your life to its fullest potential.

Time management becomes especially important as you gain bigger and bigger leadership roles, and the number of people who want to get on your calendar grows larger and larger. As much as you may want to meet with everyone, you simply can't and be effective. I learned to be discerning: Why do they want to meet? Is there another person who would be better suited to help? Can we do it over the phone versus an in-person meeting? Ask for an agenda so you can see where the time will be spent.

When planning your time, your initial focus should be on the big picture of what you want to accomplish. Otherwise, you're simply filling your calendar with activities that keep you busy, but may not move you toward achieving what matters to you. Sometimes just doing is exactly what you need, but a steady diet of activities without a bigger-picture view isn't a recipe for success.

Instead, keep an eye toward your goals and what will take you from here to there. Then, plot how to achieve your first goal and build from there. You won't be able to plot the entire journey and every step, only the direction. Work in time frames that allow you to schedule what you know. Then revisit as you can see farther and know more.

Write down your to-do list as if the tasks are an appointment on your calendar. Schedule your time to optimize your most productive hours each day. My most productive time is early in the morning. I protect this time from meetings, email, or random tasks and do the most important things during this time. Resist the temptation to take an email break or check Facebook.

As I schedule my day further, I look to see if there's a natural sequence of things to build innate efficiency to my day, especially from seven a.m. to two p.m. After two p.m., I try to schedule activities that get me moving because that time is less productive for me. I'm also careful to have a lighter schedule after noon on a Friday or before holiday breaks to allow me to clean things up before I leave. Doing so gives me a running start when I return.

# LIVE (AND LEARN) WITH INTENTION

Learning to manage your time is more art than science, so enjoy the journey, especially those places you spent time just because. Your big-picture outcome will be possible because you managed the minutes with a view toward the overall direction. But remember, going from here to there is never a direct line. The world isn't designed to help you achieve your long-term goals. You need to plan and control your environment or it will control you.

## Focus

Where you put your attention is where you'll have growth. Learning to be intentional in your focus will help accelerate your journey and your capacity to take on what lies ahead.

I've learned the value of finding time to be in my focus zone. This time allows me to be more focused and productive and slows me down a bit as I think about what is next. I try to imagine it as a wayside rest or a scenic overlook where I pull over to enjoy the view on a sunny day as I ride my motorcycle along the river. My visual gives me peace and quiets my thinking so I can think about where I want to go next. I have a choice. I can go back where I came from, stay where I am, or continue ahead. It's up to me. The same is true in your life journey.

Sometimes, these stops along the route introduce you to others or give you time to ask questions that allow you to be clearer about the next move. What's important is to keep moving. Too many times, I see people pull over in the wayside rest of life and never leave because their role isn't totally clear. Well, it never will be. Ask yourself "What is the risk of not knowing?" Most of the time, it isn't material. But not doing is. Learning to have confidence in your ability to figure it out will allow you to move on.

Think about focus as a big zoom lens on a camera. You can see where you are and can zoom into a future destination. What isn't clear is the in between. But, remember, no matter how beautiful the current view is, more scenic overlooks will be ahead. Continue on your journey and stop at the next outlook to see ahead. Doing so will allow you to go further.

As important as managing your daily time is, learning to focus on what is next and then pausing to look ahead before refocusing is critical, too. You'll be amazed at how far you can move the dial when you have your undivided attention. Focus on what you can do about something right now and have confidence that you can figure out the rest. Then you can worry about what is next.

## Boundaries

In chapter 6, I talked about the importance of understanding your framework: your experiences, filters, resources, and you facts that form the base of how you think and feel about things. Doing this work will help identify where you want to establish your boundaries. Where do you draw the line that you won't cross?

For some boundaries, drawing the line is easy. The ethics and values you hold near and dear to whom you are clarify that they aren't moveable. Others types of boundaries are less clear. Your boundaries will be tested over the course of your lifetime. You're the only one who can define and defend your boundaries. Practicing the art of defending them will show others what matters most to you and clarify to you and others what is negotiable.

Let me give you an example to illustrate the point. One afternoon at work, a senior executive I had known for years approached me. He stopped in my office and asked me if I would do a favor for him. He indicated that his wife might call me to ask if I had planned to travel with him this week. He wanted me to say yes, even though it wasn't true. I looked at him in disbelief. I told him I couldn't do that. It wasn't the truth, and I couldn't represent a plan that never existed.

I have encountered similar situations over the years, and they were never comfortable for me. But I knew if I moved my boundary once for this type of situation, it could get moved again. I needed to defend what was important to me and not be part of the situation. My boundaries simply weren't for sale.

# LIVE (AND LEARN) WITH INTENTION

Later in my career, I learned the importance of setting boundaries around scope and expectation. I love to work and figure things out. Accepting big challenges, raising the bar, and setting new standards are fun for me. However, my tremendous capacity to do work can also bring me trouble.

My mentor during my college internships first brought this to my attention. She praised me for both the quality and quantity of my work. However, she said, "You need to learn to set your own boundaries. Work will never tell you to go home, and it will always be here when you return. Your standard of work is so much higher than others, and it will become what people expect of you. It's not fair, but it will happen, trust me. Establish your boundaries, or it will have dire consequences for you later in life—personally and professionally." I must admit, I heard what she said that day, but I didn't fully understand the wisdom of this advice until many years later.

People will want you to do things in which you excel and have capacity to do. Your resolve to defend your boundaries can really get tested. Even if the organization is living in a false reality and not grounded in the context of what is needed to accomplish the goals, you need to be aware of the reality so you can invest your time and energy smartly. Allow yourself to see that even though the work brings you great joy and you know how to address the issue at hand, you can't do it all. Sometimes the organization isn't going to provide the support you need to achieve the desired outcome and allow you to stay within the boundaries you've established regarding time, responsibilities, and work/life integration.

The same is true in your personal relationships. If your love for helping others reinforces that others can always count on you to help them with this or that, you won't have time for what matters to you. Offer a little help, but then give the task or issue back to them. Doing so reinforces that they still own it.

Learning to find your boundaries and defend them is important. Remember, if you don't respect them, it will tell everyone else that they don't need to.

## Debrief

Debriefing allows you to stop the clock and reflect on an experience with 20/20 hindsight. You can examine each piece of the puzzle and learn from a broad base of knowledge without the real time emotion that occurs during the event.

I dedicated chapter 6 to this topic. The four key questions discussed there are essential: What are your key accomplishments? What are your key learnings? What could you have optimized better, knowing what you know now? What do you need to continue working on as you move forward?

Learning to take time to debrief with you in whatever time frame is important. For example, if you're in a new job or recently made a personal transition, you may want to complete a debriefing every ninety days to ensure that you're on the right track. Engage your boss or other meaningful people to share your thoughts and gather their perspectives, too. Doing so helps ensure that the key people in your life are on all on the same page as you are and that you've gathered the key learnings—both the facts and the emotion—while they're still fresh.

I have also used the debriefing process with my personal plans for my life, my marriage, and the lives of my adult children. It has led to some fascinating conversations that simply wouldn't have happened without the process. Many of the most valuable nuggets would simply have been lost or not acknowledged to the extent that they needed to be to take it to the next level. Taking time to examine and reflect on past experiences helps ensure that you harvest all the lessons from each experience before you lose them while rushing off to the next thing.

The debriefing is your document and your notes, not someone else's evaluation of you. Instead the debriefing is a collective summary of what you think is important. This distinction is critical. The notes on the paper can't be a passive collection of what others say; they're your engaged summary, which means you have processed the information and have come to some conclusions or identified some critical questions that need more thought. Collecting information from others as a point of reference is okay, but you must come to some conclusions for it to be useful in the future. Your answers will help you identify the so-what question of the experience. The net result will be a refined understanding of you and your foundation. It will help you adjust your personal governance—what you know and what you believe about you. Be open to discovering some things you must unlearn and relearn as you work to improve your self-awareness.

## Curiosity

You come into this world wired to be curious. However, as time goes on and you begin to figure things out, you focus more on the answers and less on the questions. Schools and formal education reinforce the value of the answer versus the question. Organizations push for efficiency and want everything in real time, which also is about the answers. Questions take too much time, so you stop asking them. It takes personal commitment and perseverance to nurture your ability to be curious and to practice developing these skills in the face of a world that won't help you.

I too have subscribed to getting the answer versus taking time to figure it out. It appeared that the answer would move us forward to the next thing. Sometimes I find myself annoyed at a person who was asking questions, until I learned, firsthand, the importance of asking questions and being curious.

I was in the middle of helping develop a new approach to the market. I had the good fortune to work with an industry master. As we worked together over an intense two weeks, our new direction emerged. At the time, I didn't appreciate the patience of this master as he endured my endless questions about new ideas and approaches. Never once did he stop to tell me that it wouldn't work or that he tried it before. Nor did he try to make sure I understood just who he was or remind me that I didn't have his perspective and portfolio of accomplishments. In fact, the opposite was true.

He would attack each question with the curiosity of seeing it for the first time. In fact, he always had more questions for me to ensure that he was seeing what I saw. Then together we would build on the ideas of the other person. The experience was magical. Over the years, we continued our quest for industry-leading launches and thoughtful launch plans that our teams could execute. Each time, I marveled at his curiosity and learned the value of asking good questions, listening actively, engaging by doing, asking more questions, listening again, and doing some more.

He was the embodiment of "age is just a number." Although he was more than twenty years my senior, he attacked each day with the curiosity to discover more. There was always more to learn. He simply didn't want to waste time recounting what he knew, but rather he focused his energy on the things that were left to be discovered and understood. You would do well to follow his example.

## LESSON 4

# INNOVATION STARTS WITH THE LEADER

The world today is abuzz with conversations, opinion pieces, and news stories about innovation, market disruption, and accelerated change, but what often gets missed is that innovation starts with the leader.

Innovation is personal. If you aren't innovating in your life, you aren't in a position to lead innovation. Why? Because you have forgotten what learning something new is like. You may have arrived at a place in your life where you want to be the teacher and not the student. You'll support innovation in your organization as long as it doesn't involve you, but today's marketplace demands a thorough examination of business models, investments, and resource allocations. Make no mistake; you must be engaged. There is no more business as usual where you can rinse and repeat what has worked in the past.

Leading innovation also requires an acute self-awareness of how you lead, or you'll inadvertently kill ideas before they begin. People will watch you and interpret your hallway conversation, email, or what others say in a way that will stop progress. In some cases, it may be your knee-jerk reaction to an initiative that you didn't authorize so you exercise your authority to stop it because it surprised you. In other words, your emotional fear and ego will get the best of you unless you're aware and manage it.

Innovation is a team effort that can only result from a coordinated group of activities. The team effort requires individuals to leave aside their selfish agendas to work as a team—which is why leadership is a key driver of innovation. You set the tone and reinforce the environment that will allow the organization to build its innovation fitness.

## Ten Essential Skills for Leading Innovation

Building the innovation muscle takes a lot of practice. Without the right leadership and organizational culture, innovation will never happen. Here are the ten leadership skills I consider essential to building a culture of innovation:

- Put value in the question—not just the answer.

- Be intentional in getting ideas from divergent sources and pushing critical thinking.

- Defer judgment to allow the ideas to expand and let the people figure out what is best.

- Make debriefings and assessments persistent, authentic, transparent, and *never* punitive.

- Identify key learnings and what could have been optimized—not what went wrong.

- Declare the importance of practicing to build skills and learn out loud (i.e., share and address your weaknesses or lack of knowledge with your team).

- Focus on the objectives, not the people. The objectives will unify everyone, while a focus on individual people can divide and distract the team. A collective focus is needed to get people moving in one direction.

- Celebrate forward movement and then move again.

- Prioritize what matters; do a readiness test and then pilot it in the right places, with the right people.

- Dream big, start tiny, and scale with intention.

One of the most challenging aspects of leading innovation is balancing the need to maintain the efficiency and effectiveness of your organization while also nurturing an environment that can support the messy, nonlinear process of innovation.

I love the saying, "don't bump the fishbowl," which I heard from S. Chris Edmonds when he talked about what he learned from his boss at the YMCA, Jerry Nutter. It demonstrates the unintended consequences that can happen when creating a culture of innovation. His point is that when you bump a goldfish bowl, the fish aren't happy. In fact, they scurry about and take cover out of fear. They don't know what is coming next. They're unable to go about their business anymore. You can see them huddle together, watch everything around them, and wait. The same is true of people in an organization. When something unexpected happens, they get nervous and wonder what's going to happen next.

That's why as a leader you need to intentionally engage with your teams and set the stage for innovation by proactively communicating both the purpose and context. Then make yourself available to listen so things can be implemented and changed as needed. Being clear about the purpose up front will put you and your team in a better place to pivot if things don't go as planned and will help keep the focus on the objective versus the people doing the work. Learn to embrace both the creative ideas and the failures. Not embracing the failures with a keen eye toward what you learned will discourage your employees from doing anything creative. Your intentional leadership will also make it easier for you to detect if there is any unintentional bumping of the fishbowl going on that needs your attention.

My nature is to look for innovation as a way of living my life. Remember my life's purpose: to bring relevance and high performance to a future goal. I'm not a maintainer. I live to make things better and improve the world around me so others can take it to the next level.

This perspective has allowed me to be involved in many projects and initiatives over the course of my career. I've created the previously provided list over time, and as you might imagine, many backstories support the reason for each of the ten essential skills.

My most robust story about innovation is one I mentioned earlier. I'm providing a more detailed version here because it helps illustrate the list in action. I was taking over a new role in the retail industry. The organization was profitable but struggling with growth. The value proposition was tired, and the consumer was ready for something new. It was an opportunity of a lifetime to change an organization and lead an industry.

The organization had a compliance-driven culture that was prescriptive and allowed for little opportunity to add value from the individual employee. In fact, I had never seen such a drastic example of compliance focus in my entire career. It was as if the employees had been hired for their talents, but they were told on their first day of work to give their brain to the employer for safekeeping and just follow this list of rules. Visits from the field management were focused on compliance calls and a fear of being written up.

The company needed to change in order to meet its growth expectation. I led a dedicated group of people from locations across the company who had agreed to work together to figure out what we needed to do. Our focus was on giving feedback to each other. We periodically gathered in small groups of ten to twenty people for several hours. Each person brought examples of his or her work. We shared them with each other and provided feedback, specifically what could be celebrated and what could be optimized. Then everyone went back to their locations and made changes based on the feedback, which they would bring back to the group for more feedback. We repeated this process over and over again until we felt we had an approach that would work.

When we rolled out this new approach that empowered the people, we unleashed the pride of the employees in their work. We gave them back their brains and encouraged them to add value. We taught our field management how to celebrate and move forward again. In fact, we threw away all the red pens to signal that it was no longer about finding what was wrong; it was about finding things that could be optimized.

Shortly after, I remember traveling to see a manager. During our visit, she walked over to a drawer and took out examples of her work. I loved what she was doing. In the process of the conversation, she said to me, "It's so fun to be able to talk about this kind of work and not hide it. In the past, we would get notes in our file that we weren't following the corporate model. In fact, sometimes we would have to argue with the plant to print the images because they thought it was a mistake."

They were trying to deliver value to the customer even though the organization didn't get it. Unfortunately, this problem has been true to a certain extent in every organization in which I have been a part. Many times, the disconnect is with the leadership team and the organizational middle, not the front line. In fact, the middle can operate like a Guardians of No Progress© as they protect against unnecessary risk or things that don't fit the mold. It takes your leadership engagement to lead them out and model a new way.

As we practiced our new employee-empowered approach, making sure that we brought our field leadership teams along was important. The leaders were learning right alongside their teams. This was new to them, so it was uncomfortable. They had come from a place where management always knew the answers. Now that was no longer true. We had to make it safe for them to learn, too. Their reputations and sense of pride were at stake. That is where we created a name for our process of Learn Out Loud. This process put the focus on practice and learning together so we could demonstrate that 1 + 1 = 3. When they didn't know how to approach something, we challenged them to "when in doubt, make it up." Then we always ended the session with a celebrate and move focus. Focusing on key learnings and moving forward allowed the management team members to accelerate their cycle of learning, practicing, and celebrating, which delivered historic new results. This built a new mojo for the team and a new competency, which allowed us to forever change an industry.

None of this required more money from the organization. The only thing required was a new focus on our most precious resources—our human capital and our time. It required a tremendous involvement by the leader and the leadership team to engage fully to make it happen. Our walk, not our talk, ultimately moved the dial.

Your ability to be intentional in your leadership is what will make innovation possible. Make no mistake. But don't forget your senior leadership. Depending on your structure, getting them engaged and moving innovation forward can be a bigger challenge. They aren't in the front line. If they live by what they can see only on the financial reports, your ability to move forward will be limited if not impossible. The final outcome will depend on the same elements that I talked about earlier. Are they innovating in their personal lives? Can they provide balanced leadership that maintains the necessary efficiency/effectiveness of the organization while creating space for innovation to occur? The answer to both ultimately must be yes, or the organization will be hindered. Even if you get everything moving right, they can bump your fishbowl and stop forward movement. Building the alignment and opening communication is important so this process is acknowledged and supported.

And don't forget the three approaches that I discussed earlier—learn out loud, when in doubt make it up, and celebrate and move. They are missing elements in most innovation initiatives, especially if there is immense pressure to increase numbers. Everyone starts making shortcuts and moving toward what is safe and efficient, which kills the long-term innovation efforts.

And innovation is essential to optimize a bright future. However, it's also a high-risk role if the right leadership at all levels of the organization doesn't support it.

# LESSON 5

# DON'T SKIP RUNGS ON THE LADDER TO SUCCESS

*A*s I stated earlier, true mastery takes ten thousand hours, which amounts to five years of dedicated work. Understanding the experience needed to build skills and capacity to lead is critical. Otherwise you will inadvertently skip a step that will be a career stopper later in your career.

Managing your career with stops along the way to check the box of the next required job title won't serve you well. It will detour you off the mastery path and you'll miss the rewards available when you leverage your time in a designated area. A check-the-box resume will also raise questions by hiring managers regarding your motivation, skill level, on-the-job engagement, and ability to get along with other colleagues.

Your development as a leader requires time. You can't master it in a day by taking a course or reading a book. You can only do it by dedicating the time to learn and practice skills and to gain an understanding of what you must value and learn on each step of your career ladder.

Let me say that again. Your development as a leader requires time.

There are simply no shortcuts if you want to build a foundation that can support and sustain your future leadership aspirations. Period.

Your skill development is dependent on not skipping a step or moving too quickly. You need to focus on the right priorities, in the right order, at the right pace. Sometimes the best option is to take a lateral move to build a stronger base of experience or even take a step back to get on a different path that offers more opportunity. Remember that you're trying to build capacity and competency, not a list of job titles.

Realizing that development can happen in your current role is also important. On my first job, one of my assignments was to be a technical writer for job descriptions that used the Hay system for compensation. It was a very programmed way to write, but it also was a discipline that ensured crystal clarity for the organization. I didn't appreciate the discipline or the perspective I was learning at the time. However, I have used this perspective to understand every organization and position I have held and am forever grateful for the experience. It has helped ensure alignment, reduce duplication, and bring a focus to why positions/departments/functions exist and what the expectations are for results. I have been amazed at the amount of time I have spent in this fundamental area over the years as I moved to more senior roles.

**Different Jobs, Different Priorities**

From a big-picture perspective, your first job will be focused on your individual contributions, your reliability, and the way you fit into the company values and culture. The most senior job will be focused on the entire organization and how the total operating system works to deliver value. Learning to navigate the career ladder from bottom to top will help you accelerate your growth and achieve full performance at all leadership levels. However, your ability to move up and thrive will be directly related to your alignment with what is valued at each level: specifically, what do you value, what brings you joy, and what makes you proud?

As a newer employee, the contribution that will attract the most attention and consideration for a potential leadership role is your ability to take on more responsibility. Then, as you move into a leadership role, it will be about your ability to shift from doing the work to working with others to get the work done. I have seen this transition stump people. They just can't get out of their own way. They value their own work above everyone else, and doing the actual work brings them so much joy that they want to stay involved. They're proud of what they've done because they know no one can do it better.

But remember, true leadership is about others. If you don't enjoy working with others, focus your efforts on being an expert, specialist, or other highly valued individual contributor role. These roles line up more appropriately with what matters to you—what you value, what brings you joy, and what makes you proud.

If, on the other hand, you value others, get joy from working with them to get results, and are proud of your collective team effort, then you have the potential to thrive at the next level. At this point, you're not only developing yourself; you're putting your attention on developing others. You must be able to discern those who do from those who can lead. Learning to be an effective coach who provides real-time feedback to help your team members improve is critical.

I had to learn this skill on my own. There weren't many resources to help me see what good coaching looked like so I could follow a the role model and then make it my own. Instead, I learned from trial and error and watching it done poorly or not at all. Later in my career, I supported training efforts to make it possible to build this capability across the enterprise.

**Being an Effective Coach**

Learning to be an effective coach is an essential skill for any leader. Yelling louder isn't a winning coaching model. Understanding what type of coaching is needed for each person is the critical ingredient. Remember the power of my sons' lacrosse coach in chapter 1. His ability to change his approach to meet what each of my boys needed to go forward was the difference maker.

This is an area where I think leaders waste tremendous human potential. The employer/coach only knows one way to do the job, and if it doesn't fit the employee, their performance is limited. The net result is frustration, lost energy, and diminished, not optimized, potential. This is typical when the boss only knows how to be stern with the feedback, point out all that is wrong, or focus on how the numbers aren't at goal.

This type of coaching is typical with younger managers and supervisors because they think bosses are supposed to act this way or they live in an environment that shows them that this behavior is needed to be tough. It may be "tough," but it's not effective. In my experience, what's effective is providing positive reinforcement, celebrating what is right, debriefing to identify issues, and making adjustments that reflect the talents and growth areas of each individual, as well as the team as a whole. Bottom line, one size doesn't fit all. If you're going to lead, you need to find the form of coaching that best fits each employee, not the other way around.

As a side note, if you're a person who needs encouragement or coaching to help you see a better way, realize that you'll never thrive in a tough talk environment. You'll either need to figure out a way to self-coach, grow a hard shell and learn to survive, or develop an exit strategy while learning whatever you can from the situation.

## Higher Levels of Leadership

As you move to the next levels of leadership, you'll be required to expand your scope of responsibility to areas outside your expertise. You'll also need to build your proficiency in strategy and blend it with your functional expertise. You'll be expected to compete for resources, while also, somewhat paradoxically, strengthen your ability to play as a team. In addition, you'll need to learn how to communicate through levels of management down to the front line to ensure the message is understood, but without overriding your management team. You'll thrive in this type of role if you value a diverse team, are skilled at looking ahead and aligning the pieces to work together, and enjoy celebrating the success of your team's accomplishments.

After you move to the executive suite or a general manager role, your focus will shift to the integration of functions and balancing future and present needs. You'll need to value and build trust with all organizational functions to inspire contribution from all areas of the business. Reserving time to work on the business by designating thinking time on your calendar versus facing a full calendar of doing will be critical. You'll thrive in this role if you can value the overall business success, enjoy building a business, and take pride in the collective success.

Finally, as you arrive at the C-suite, you must learn to truly value the success of others and celebrate their accomplishments. Your coaching role focuses on business leaders, and your energy is around evaluating strategy, asking the right questions, considering capital and resource allocation/deployment, and the core capabilities of your business to meet the current and future expectations. You'll need to build expertise to see around the corners for long-term thinking about where you're headed, be clear about what is required of your overall system to deliver, and know what tradeoffs you must make or consider to optimize the results of the collective business. This role will challenge you to know how things work, or should work, to support what needs to be done. It will tap your curiosity, your ability to ask questions, and your skill at building both a current reality and a future so you can see around the corners and chart the course.

**What Matters in Every Job**

As you move from one spot to the next, make sure you value what matters at each step. If not, you won't thrive and, in fact, you can do more harm. In my experience, I've referred to those who move to a position that is out of alignment with their values as arsonists. These people do things that actually work against the organization. They're dangerous because they're part of the team—technically—but not in their actions. In some cases they actually get credit for jumping in to help with the fires that inevitably happen in an organization—until it becomes clear that they're the ones who started the fire. Be on the lookout for arsonists so that you don't praise them, but rather get to the root of the fire that can endanger the entire organization.

Two fundamental dimensions matter for every job. First, be clear about the role, goal, and deliverables of the position. Second, be clear about the magic three—authority, accountability, and responsibility. Most importantly, make sure that they're all aligned for what you need to get the job done. If any of them are out of alignment or not clear, your ability to be successful will be compromised. Don't assume anything. Always take time to determine the fundamentals of each job.

What you typically see is that once you get the roles, goals, and deliverables clear, one of the magic three are out of alignment. For example, you can see that the job has the responsibility to deliver XYZ, but you don't have the accountability or authority to make it happen. Or you have the responsibility and accountability but lack the authority to make it happen. Take the time to work through the details of your role so it's clear to you, your boss, and everyone else.

Be intentional about your launch into the new position. You may be totally new to the organization. Or, in some cases, you were part of the team and are now the leader. In others, you may be rejoining an organization you once were part of, but at a different level or capacity. Take advantage of your newness to get established in this new role and connect with the key peer group and stakeholders.

Don't assume this will happen by itself. Develop a plan so you leave nothing to chance. Your job as a leader is to work with people to get results. They need to be on the same page with you. Don't let them fill in the blanks from what they once knew of you (or heard of you) to what they think they see in the new role. Work with them so that you're certain they're connecting the right dots. If you sense some inaccurate perceptions, address them immediately so they don't get in the way of the success of you or your team. Make it your job to set a new stage and get them on board for where you're going together so you both start from the same place.

Your ability to change roles and make good choices will be directly related to how well you know yourself and how you align what matters to you with what matters to the position you hold. More specifically, you need to understand the answers to the value questions as well as the following. Which do you like more: Working alone or working with others? Celebrating your individual success or the success of your team? Doing the work or leading the work?

The answers to these important questions will help you gauge whether your aspirations align with what matters to you.

# LESSON 6

# FOCUS ON THE FUTURE, BUT DON'T FORGET THE FUNDAMENTALS

*A*s you've evolved into a world where everything is at play, you can easily get lost or decide that you'll wait until everything is clear. (**Hint:** It's never going to happen.)

As a leader, you need to recognize and develop the competencies you will need for future success—even when it's not completely clear. But you also need to understand and nurture the foundational competencies your company needs to survive and thrive right now. Too many times, I have seen organizations get so excited about where they're going that the basic disciplines start to decay. At first, no one notices. Then something dire happens and people wonder how it happened and why no one said anything.

Communication is an important example. After electronic communication arrived, the focus switched to how to use these exciting new tools, and the need for basic communication skills fell by the wayside. But strong communication remains vital in any organization. It's up to you, as a leader, to articulate what skills are needed—both the foundational and the shiny new skills—to remain successful.

When something new arrives on the scene, declare what won't be changing so your people know where to stand. Otherwise they won't understand what they can count on to support them while they build their new skills and organizational competency. Doing so can cause a lack of confidence that can bog down the whole organization.

While clarifying the fundamentals—what won't change—you must also make clear that change and evolution must happen. Painting the big picture is fine, but you won't move forward unless you break the steps down into meaningful chunks so people can engage and begin the journey. Deconstructing your strategic plan so you can understand how it impacts your human capital is vitally important. Without the right people and skills, you won't be able to take an organization from here to there. Thinking you can get it done simply by moving the old out and bringing in the new is misguided.

I have had the good fortune over the course of my career to lead many business transformations. In each case, I came into a situation created by others before me. I needed to respect their work while moving the organization to a new reality. The bottom line in every situation: I had to meet the organization where it was and then work to take it into the future.

Learning to take inventory of what is required for the journey is an essential step. Assessing the current status is equally important in order to identify the gaps—yours and the organization's—and the time you have to build the skill.

In one case, the organization I joined hadn't evaluated its marketing structure in sixteen years! Is it any surprise that the skills weren't there to meet the new demands of the marketplace? As leader, I easily could have thrown up my arms, taken out a white sheet of paper, and started fresh with everything. That was tempting, I must admit.

However, it was more important to unpack the bags and discover where we were, what we needed going forward, and what we didn't need to do anymore. We were able to identify the high-potential employees who were interested in an accelerated development plan as well as areas in which we needed to bring in talent from outside the company because we didn't have enough time to develop the talent inside. We needed the jump-start that experience would bring us. Their experience, with the right structure and people development plan, would allow us to execute and build momentum for the future.

Learning to use this same process for you personally is also vital. As your career grows from doing to managing, your personal skills can become outdated. Doing your own due diligence about your current skill set and the skills needed for the future is essential.

I grew up with a sales and marketing background. When I started my career, the internet didn't exist, nor did the power of social media. After they arrived on the scene, I needed to develop my own personal development plan to keep up. I continue to monitor my online and social media skills and other new areas, starting with where I am and then moving to where I think I need to be in these areas.

Over the course of my career, emerging areas that required new skill development for me and my executive team included cybersecurity, the transition of film to digital, and the move to total systems thinking. The evolution of your leadership and your competencies isn't optional. You can't hide behind bureaucracy; you must be actively engaged to make this happen.

Just as the Industrial Age taught efficiency, what is now being called the Social Age is teaching transparency. As leaders, it's important to be transparent about your need to keep learning. It builds trust with your team and empowers them to notice marketplace changes and develop the skills needed to address those changes. Learning to make the lifelong commitment to be disciplined in this area is vital for your future. Too many times, I meet very successful people who suddenly find themselves on the outside looking in because they haven't developed the skills they need to remain viable in their current position. Some find other opportunities in their organizations. But others are transitioned out. The marketplace can be brutal. If you have experience as a leader but lack the skills needed in today's marketplace, finding your next place can be difficult.

On the other hand, you may find yourself in an organization that isn't keeping pace with what needs to happen, so the opportunity to be engaged in key advancements is limited. Only you can assess whether you can stay up-to-date by seeking projects or engagements outside the organization and remain in your current role, or whether it's best to move on.

Long term, if the organization doesn't take steps forward, it, too, will face a challenged future. Take the time to assess whether the organization is just slow to start or whether there is no appetite to move forward. It's tough for any organization to be on the cutting edge of all new development, so learning to gauge the context of your organization and your ability to develop will be critical.

# LESSON 7

# EMBRACE DIVERSITY

*I* remember the summer of 1981 like it was yesterday. A friend and I were headed to Washington DC, for internships at the US Department of Justice. It was an opportunity of a lifetime.

The day of departure, my friend and I packed my Firebird Formula full to the brim before setting out for the long drive to American University, where the dorms would be filled with interns for the summer. We arrived after spending twenty-two hours on the road—we didn't want to waste our money on a hotel room for the night. The excitement of being back in the city was electric. I had been in Washington DC, the previous January for a one-month stay to study government. It, too, was a magical time, as we were able to be part of Ronald Reagan's presidential inauguration.

This time I would spend ten weeks immersed in the city, national events, and the sea of historical sites. As a group of poor college students, we found clever ways to save money and still be part of the action. It was a wonderful time, and yet some days, I felt alone. For the first time in my life, I felt part of the minority because I was different.

In my hometown, diversity was defined by which church you attended or whether you lived in town or on the farm. But at least to me, we all looked the same. Now I worked and lived with a much more diverse group. It was a melting pot of skin color, cultural norms, and histories. There was a broad and diverse perspective on how to live life.

I learned to embrace diversity and inclusion as a point of strength where 1 + 1 could equal 3. To make this possible, I needed to be aware of how my identity, cultural norms, heritage, and history could shape my relationship with others. At the same time, I needed to be open to new ideas and ways of thinking, and value multiple perspectives so I could approach things from a mind-set of collaboration, continuous learning and reflection, and opinions based on exploration and evidence.

My curiosity about how and why others thought what they did has been a key focus of mine ever since those early days. I could see how the bias in my own family might color my perspective. I took extra steps to study the lessons of history, understand people's life stories, and expose myself to things that sometimes were uncomfortable. From visits to the Auschwitz concentration camp in Germany and the Museum of Indifference in Los Angeles to taking time to talk with students and staff in schools across America, I made time to explore the gifts and tragedies of diversity so I could build my skills as a leader and bring others with me.

This skill is growing in importance. Today's organizations are the most diverse in history—by generation, ethnicity, gender, and more. If you desire your organization to be more competent in dealing with diversity, you must develop your skills first and then live them out loud so you can foster them in others. By knowing your cultural norms, values, and attitudes, you can focus on the skills and behaviors necessary to embrace the realities of the global world.

Changing others' perspectives is more difficult. I'm still amazed at the ongoing conversation about women in leadership, as if it's still a novelty. I would hope that by now the world can move beyond this issue. Why are people not focused on the issues that need to be solved? Instead, so many people seem to want to put labels on people based on how they're "packaged" on the outside versus what they can contribute from the inside.

Diversity is a focus I try to keep front and center. A friend framed it best. Diversity can only be embraced when we put it "at" the table, not "on" the table. I agree. If people can use our leadership to focus on the issues at hand and then work to ensure that the right people are at the table to solve them, people can move forward. The results have and will demonstrate the value in this approach.

In the end, it's about your ability to develop the adaptability and collaborative capabilities to allow individuals and organizations to integrate and use a collective approach. You can't live as silos. The world is too interconnected now. The successful organizations will have diverse teams that can identify and communicate the points of connection—shared goals, priorities, and values—that transcend their differences and enable them to build relationships and to work together.

Part of this process is learning how you show up and taking the time to acknowledge your historical roots and their effect on you. Everyone comes with accepted norms from their family, community, culture, and gender. Unfortunately, Caucasians are the one group that doesn't take the time to acknowledge this as part of them. They identify these issues with race and therefore don't acknowledge their own cultural norms because they believe they don't have a culture, but everyone does.

What is your inner sense of who you are? What are the socially constructed ideals, scripts, and expectations of how you express yourself and behave? Who does what, when, and how? Answering these questions will help you understand your own context and how it affects your thoughts and actions. Only then can you truly understand why others may think and act differently from you and why you shouldn't see this difference as alarming, but rather as something that will enrich you and your organization.

# LESSON 8

# RELATIONSHIPS MATTER–MAKE THEM A PRIORITY

*I* credit living in a small town with teaching me the value of relationships. In a weird way, it was great preparation for the world I live in today, where everyone is connected.

My small town had only 832 people. Many of the families were multigenerational, often with long histories among families and between individuals. My small town newspaper recorded all the events of town. During college, my subscription to the *Gibbon Gazette* was mailed to me every Thursday. My friends would come over to see what had been happening. We were enamored with the "Social Scene," a section of the paper that reported who entertained guests in their homes and what they did—kind of like today's modern-day social media. Every week, we could count on reading about Neva Kiecker and a few others. But like a popular page on Facebook, Neva was whom everyone followed. She lived down the street from me, attended my church, and was a classmate of my great aunt.

My small town was also the kind of place where everyone knew his or her address—because snail mail needed a return address—but didn't pay much attention to anyone else's address. People just knew where others lived and how to get there. A street address wasn't useful for most purposes. But one day, as my friend and I were walking through town, an ambulance headed to an emergency stopped us to ask where an address was located. Neither of us had any idea, so we asked if they knew the name of the person. They did, so we could point them in the right direction.

In my hometown, the relationships that we created, developed, and nurtured over time determined how we worked, how we related to each other, and how we contributed to the community. The same is true today. However, I worry that the art of engaging in a truly authentic human experience gets lost in modern-day communication. Just take a look around you and see the number of people who are on their cell phones versus engaging with the people and experiences around them. That, in turn, affects your ability to build trust with each other, communicate effectively, and work out your issues.

That's why, when I started serving on boards, I made it a priority to go out for a meal with every board member over the course of my term. During the meal, I learned more about that member, what made him or her tick, why he or she was on the board, and our common interests or connections. Could I learn this by looking at the board members' bios, LinkedIn profiles, and whatever I could find on Google? Sure, but it isn't the same. We wouldn't have a relationship; I would simply have more knowledge about a person I could call a colleague. A great place to begin to have the conversation with someone is to learn more about his or her inside story—and then you can begin to build a relationship.

I remember meeting with a young professional who had yet to learn this lesson. He had reached out to me to discover more about my career and get ideas for his future. I asked him whether he belonged to any trade associations, had attended any events that featured prominent leaders, or had gone to any industry conventions. He looked puzzled and asked why those were important. I told him that I had attended many such events over the course of my career and found them very useful for developing my knowledge and skills.

To which he said, "Well I do that too, but I go to YouTube. You know, you can find anything you want there, and you can get it when you need it." He said this as if it would be a news flash for me. But that's not what stopped me in my tracks. I realized that he placed no value in the experience of meeting new people. To him, the world was his oyster as long as he had his computer.

But building relationships takes time and dedication. There are no shortcuts. Your organizations, your titles, your activities—the outside story—will all change. Relationships are the only thing that will endure time. Make it a priority to seek them out and build them authentically.

Social media has made connecting with people easier, but not always authentic. I remember a time when I was approached on LinkedIn with what appeared at first to be a personal message, but it was actually a sales message camouflaged to look like it came from a friend. I'm not looking for that kind of connection. The art of building a relationship in order to understand the other person, his or her needs, and issues is the essence of this human experience called life, yet I'm afraid that this art has been lost.

The relationship isn't just about you. It's about being real, transparent, and engaged with another person with no expectations of a return. It's about building relationships that are fueled by curiosity and a willingness to learn more about you and others. When you find you need another set of eyes, a quick touch base, or just a break in the action, you'll have a strong network to call on for help. And vice versa. Your network will also be the people who will help you build a better self-awareness because they know you and feel comfortable sharing feedback.

Asking for feedback is a good practice, most of the time. Remember, people are wired to fill in their mental voids with the negative side of the story, so asking others for help filling them in is important. However, do be cautious about whom you approach. You need to approach people who have a real experience with you, not someone who knows you superficially because he or she got most of his or her information about you from others. Just as I experienced in my small town, you build your reputation by establishing yourself one person at a time and then by working to ensure you proactively manage the relationship. Your reputation, no matter the setting, is developed using the social skills and emotional intelligence to be a better leader.

As you rise in the organization and become the leader, this skill is even more important because lots of people will want to fill in the blanks for you and about you. You can't do anything to stop them from doing it; however, you can make it a practice to be authentically engaged so people get to know you. They'll then have less of a void to fill in and in some cases, they may feel more comfortable about coming to you to fill in the blanks versus taking other people's word for it.

I learned to tell all my direct reports and sometimes reports a few levels down that if anyone comes to them and tries to move things forward with the directive of "Nancy says" that they should throw a yellow flag. Then come to me and touch base. Having people come to me gives an opportunity to learn two things. First, I learn which people have to leverage my name to get something done versus relying on their own leadership ability. Second, I learn how what I did or didn't say was being translated throughout the organization.

Both are very valuable lessons. The first one could mean that a team member might need some extra effort and coaching in order to feel he or she can move a project forward. Or it might signal that the change you're leading is hitting unexpected resistance and needs to be reexamined to ensure the right outcome. Team members who do something just because the leader says so don't allow themselves to add value. To get the best outcome, people need to engage at every step and not abdicate their role because the leader said. The team needs to identify and share key learnings with you along the way. Make it clear to your team that this expectation is yours and not a sign of defiance to your leadership; it's a sign of strength and health of the team.

As I mentioned, the second learning allows me to see how my messages are being interpreted and translated into action. As a leader, you can feel like a broken record, repeating the same message over and over. But as I discussed earlier, people learn differently. You need to repeat your messages in many different forms to ensure everyone hears the message. Feedback given directly to you helps you see this in real time and helps you fine-tune your leadership impact and accelerate your learning alongside your people.

## Managing Relationships

Over time, you develop an understanding of each relationship so you know how to manage it. Some people will forever be just a colleague. You know each other and a little about each other's story. You share something in common, but not enough to actively manage the relationship. You would take a call from this person or answer an email, but it's not likely you'd put a note in your calendar to schedule a follow-up meeting.

On the other end of the spectrum are people who you want to be back in contact with at some date in the future. I have found that making a list and actively managing how often I want to see certain people is the only way to make sure I do it. If I leave it to chance, too much time will pass and seeing them simply won't happen. Or it will happen so infrequently that it doesn't allow me to elevate my relationship with a person. Learning to do this simple step took me a while, but doing it has made all the difference. It letting go as you get busy with life is easy. My simple advice is don't let this happen. Investing your time and energy to engage more deeply in your network is always a wise investment. Learning to do it on an ongoing basis takes discipline and intention.

# LESSON 9

# LEVERAGE COLLABORATIONS AND STRATEGIC PARTNERS

*O*rganizations with rigid command and control structures are becoming vulnerable to competition from short-term collaborations and longer-lasting strategic partnerships. This new reality will attack every corner of society—from corporations to government to education and beyond.

As a leader, this new reality challenges you to think about what your organization does, what you can outsource, and where you can engage strategic partners. Think about it. Today, Uber, the world's largest ride-sharing service, owns no vehicles. Facebook, the world's most popular content provider, creates no content. Other companies like eBay, LinkedIn, TripAdvisor, and Priceline also don't own what people do on their site. In every case, these companies have created an experience that solves a problem for the end user—getting a ride, staying connected, selling/buying something they have or want, planning a vacation. They minimized the overhead and focused on the customer interface and experience.

The advantage to companies that were vertically integrated (i.e., they owned every part of their supply chain) is being erased and being replaced with the power of the customer relationship that builds when the customer easily can solve his or her issue. The shift of power is moving from what—the end product that customers want—to how companies address their customer needs. The infrastructure that once was only available in organizations is now available to anyone who can leverage alliances and strategic partnerships. When there's no rigid corporate structure to navigate, a different relationship can be formed with the end user, and the value chain can be more agile. Building your organization's capacity to develop collaborations and strategic partnerships will be critical to your ability to be both agile and nimble in the marketplace.

Your organization is built to be efficient in doing your business. Your people are focused on protecting what is important to the organization. But if what's important is changing, their diligence can slow things down and even cause opportunities to be lost because your team doesn't get it. Staying connected to your team is vital to ensure that as the marketplace changes and your company changes, your people change with it.

I recently attended an Innovation Conference with leaders who lead change initiatives and strategic partnerships every day. Everyone talked about the struggle to get new ideas, new business models, and new solutions launched. Strategic partnerships are built on trust and are high risk. Everyone is watching—in many cases, both externally and internally—so a lot is at stake, up to and including your job. Your team will need to exercise due diligence to protect themselves and your organization. Taking time to ensure your team understands why this is important and, more important, what is at stake, is vital.

The marriage of your company foundation, your outside entrepreneurs, and your inside entrepreneurs will make this happen. When the partnership hits your team's radar, it's easy to get lost in the scalability, the strength or size of your partner, the ROI, etc. Sometimes, the strategic partnership is about getting something new started, and these questions can't be answered until you do something with the idea.

At the conference, I loved hearing how 3M transformed its thinking about ideas and how to handle them. Here I'm paraphrasing the 3M speaker: "We get approached all the time with ideas. I have been involved in many of these conversations for thirty-five years. In the beginning, the conversation always started with a discussion of ownership—what we own that will contribute to the idea's success and how to handle ownership of the new product or process that will result. Now we focus on the issue that needs to be solved and the resulting business opportunity. Everything else is secondary. We know that we can't do it on our own. We need a strong and robust process to vet the people and organizations bringing ideas from outside 3M to identify their potential as partners. These skills and the power of your network will become new foundational skills needed by any organization to stay relevant."

I see this as one of the greatest opportunities that any generation has ever faced—to completely remake the world without the artificial boundaries of an organization—to truly focus on the customer experience and interface to make solutions possible. The curiosity of the new generation to understand the why will focus the conversation on what matters to the customer instead of just perpetuating what has been done in the past.

# LESSON 10

# SEE AROUND THE CORNERS AND SHARE THE VIEW

*L*eaders see around the corners and connect the dots in ways that makes sense of everything. When a leader explains, "Here's why this happened," it makes sense to you and leaves you wondering why you didn't see it too. You didn't because seeing the big picture—the many parts that make up the full context of a situation—isn't always easy.

When leaders are faced with difficult challenges, they do not surrender. Instead, they dig deeper to understand the framework and context so they can see the full view. This allows the leaders and their teams to redefine their future and optimize the journey ahead. That is when you know you are working for a leader versus a manager.

I have worked with both types in my career. Unfortunately, I have had more managers than true leaders. The distinction between managers and leaders is in how they attack their work. A manager works in the business and focuses on what comes at them. A leader works on the business by looking ahead and being proactive. They still focus on what matters today, but always with an eye towards what is coming next. Both managers and leaders have taught me lessons, but the leaders who took time to help me understand context showed me the importance of this discipline.

Whether creating a plan for a new endeavor or tackling "what went wrong" with a past project, leaders who know how to ask questions, flush out the alternatives, and connect the dots are able create a new reality alongside their teams. Executives who passively engage and occasionally "check in" with their team won't be successful in the long run. The broader view is needed as the team works to address issues. If you leave everything to the updates, you will lose your ability to really see and hear what's happening.

I had the opportunity to be tested on this when I assumed a new role at a company. The results had been flat for several years and there was concern for the future of the business. My focus was to see if there was something that could be done to ignite growth. It took nearly ten weeks of travel on the road to understand the context of the business and the real issues that faced the team.

I remember returning with new insights and lots of questions. I wanted to verify that what I was seeing was reality, so I booked several meetings with key members of the home office team. When I asked one of them to help me understand what was happening, he shook his head and looked back at me.

I will never forget what he said: "Nancy, you just don't understand. You are new and see all the dead bodies lying on the floor. We have lived here for so long that we know where they are, so we just step over them to get our jobs done."

Wow, what do you say to that response?

The people had been beaten down and told to focus on the job. They did as they were told. No one was working alongside them to understand the issues and build a plan to enable them to redefine their futures. Doing the same thing harder isn't going to yield different results.

By bringing my team of fifteen together to frame the context of the current business and outline a future reality, we were able to get people engaged to drive new results. We took time to see what was happening in the world around us, to learn how what we did fit in the world, and to understand why it mattered, so we could do something about it. It gave the bigger group a better understanding of our mission, their role, and specifically what needed to get done to drive a different future. The time we spent together energized the team. The early pace was slow, but it picked up momentum as people learned a new way to operate and could really see where they could go.

As a leader, you have to remember, your organization cannot BE what it cannot see. Remember life is the ultimate experience model. Your people have to be able to try things on so they can begin to see new ways to do things. As they "try things on," you need to give them permission to fail or the "trying on" will stop. To make forward progress, you, as a leader, need to ensure this happens for your organization.

Contrast that with a different type of experience. Once again, I had taken on a new role and had the opportunity to learn the business. This time I found active engagement in understanding the context of the another section of organization, but no efforts to understand the bigger picture of the organization and its place in the world. This had been going on for some time. The misalignment was mind blowing and so was the waste of valiant efforts that didn't move the organization forward.

We needed a collective view. The issues facing the business were messy and complex, especially because some of the issues were a result of marketplace changes and the inability (or lack of interest) of current leadership to see around the corner. I knew stitching this mess into a forward-looking plan would be difficult, but it was still possible if the executive team members were willing to face the fact that they had built a false reality and needed to get personally engaged alongside their teams.

After some time, I left that organization. Although the leadership team members made attempts to learn about the new reality, they were unwilling to do the work to understand how to address the issues collectively and personally engage to move it forward, which made a new reality impossible. As I said before, doing the same thing harder isn't going to yield different results.

I learned later that a long-time employee asked for an exit interview with the top leader. During the course of the conversation, the employee shared his concern for the future. The top leader paused, looked the employee straight in the eyes, and said, "Yes, those are all issues that will need to be solved, but that will be someone else's job." Unbelievable. Faced with difficult circumstances, this top executive had surrendered, and the organization was caught in the riptide.

People instinctively understand that no group achieves anything worthwhile without someone in charge. That's why, especially in a crisis, people will inevitably rally around a leader. When there is no leader or one who isn't engaged, the team will work to do it on its own, but will lack the full context to solve the problem.

Remember that in today's context everything is more open, more connected, and more available to individuals than ever before. In early times, a leader could look at the workforce as his or her workforce—the employees belonged to the organization. Now, because of changes in how employees view their employers, think of employees as volunteers. Your employees easily can be aware of other opportunities and how your workplace stacks up against alternatives. Succeeding in this challenging new environment requires leaders to earn their leadership every day and understand that their authority is a short-lived phenomenon. It's their ability to build context and influence that will engage others in the mission of the organization.

Some leaders will see this new reality as a damnable constraint to their effectiveness. Great leaders will see the opportunity to gather information more easily and communicate more in real time so everyone can stay on the same page and be highly engaged. Even with less control, a leader's opportunity to be effective is greater than any other time in history. Your ability to understand the context of your organization, the reality of the marketplace, and your appetite and readiness to tackle the challenges are essential. It will take alignment of all three to drive your organization forward.

# EPILOGUE

*I*t was a day in late April when I met a friend to tell her that I was finally ready to write this book. It was a fun conversation. As we stood up to leave, she shared with me that writing the book was only 20 percent of the work. I must admit that wasn't what I wanted to hear. I hadn't written one word yet.

But after three months to organize my endless piles of ideas into my writer's grid, two months to get feedback on the concept from potential readers, four months to write the book, almost a year to finish the editing, and four months to finally publish the book, I understand the wisdom in her words.

It was a long journey and full of new learnings. After all, I had never done this before, so it took extra time to figure things out. It required me to go bump in the night and fight the temptation to give up because it was so hard. The voice in my head challenged me to consider whether it was worth it and whether it would matter. I knew if it was going to be done, I wanted to do it right. My speed wasn't the goal; I wanted to produce a product that added value to the lives of the reader. So I learned to practice patience.

And with the gift of time there is a treasure, isn't that true? The time allowed me to spend more time to refine the stories, practice the approach in new settings, and build my mastery of being grounded. The diligence in the editing process forced me to be clear even when I was sure that I had done it. In this process you create an experience for the reader so the focus is on the message and not the process of reading.

Writing this book also challenged me to walk my talk of bringing a talented group together to get their feedback. It required me to truly listen, embrace their perspective, and refine my approach. Saying and doing this are two entirely different things—another easy-to-say-hard-to-do thing in life. The subject was personal; however, the impact was designed to be universal, working to be clear about why I wrote the book, who was my target, and what was my expectation of the book took time. The process of who to assemble was critical. Everybody can make a difference in the world but no one can do it alone. The book needed the diversity to explore the edges of the message. Yet it needed the ability to collaborate and build on each other's perspectives. It needed the time to invest in really reading the manuscript and the time to ponder the message. And it needed leaders who could participate but not in their own self-interest. It helped me practice humility, leverage diversity, and embrace the potential of this book to the greater good.

I want to thank the many people who inspired this book. First to the leaders who helped me shape my approach to life: Betty Brandt, who believed in my leadership before I did and pushed me to raise the bar on what is possible; Gary Sassenberg, who inspired me to understand the power of the spoken word and the importance of stage presence; Linda Rongistch, who taught me anything is possible if you unlearn what you know and have the courage to explore what is possible; and Tom Hollaran, who showed me the wisdom of time and the importance of putting things in the right order.

Next to the leaders who shared their perspective and inspired mine: Karen Bohn, Jacqueline Byrd, PhD., Jim Campbell, Cindy Chandler, Ram Charan, Richard Davis, Sandra Davis, Matthew Dean, Debbie DiGiacomo, Seth Godin, Dr. MayKao Hang, Sue Hawkes, Karen Himle, Tom Hollaran, Udaiyan Jatar, Linda Keene, David Koentopf, Doug Lennick, Dick Lewis, David Lyman, Chris LaVictoire Mahi, Pam Moret, John Parker, Sheila Riggs, Jeannine M. Rivet, Becky Roloff, Piyumi Samaratunga, John Segall, Cecily Sommers, Dee Thibodeau, and Charlie Westerling. Your ability to bring clarity to issues, challenge me to leave nothing to chance, walk your talk as an example for others to follow, and get your hands dirty to truly understand was profound. It made the message and me forever stronger.

And lastly to the insights from my beta readers. Thank you to Dave Deal, Jan Haeg, David Hakensen, Lori Larson, Amy Langer, Tammie Lynn, Cathy Paper, Kelsie Schmit, Kathi Tunheim PhD., and Grayce Belvedere Young for your dedication to read the rough edited version and provide your feedback. Your perspectives individually and collectively added dimension to the story and the ultimate impact of the message.

Thank you for the calls to check in and sincere interest in my progress and willingness to help goes to Jay Brettingen, Stefanie Ann Lenway, Dan Mallin, David McNally, Mary Meehan, Lee Opdahl, Jeff Prouty, Anne Pryor, Eric Schneider, V.J. Smith, David Stillman, and LuAnn Via.

And this list of thanks wouldn't be complete without recognizing the support of my husband, Brian, and my boys, Erik and Jorgen. The love we share is uncompromising and recognizes that it requires us to embrace the adventures of each other, because we know it will bring joy, even if it doesn't make sense to us at the time. We know it will as we look back on our lives, but we must live it going forward. Thank you for embracing this idea and supporting my work even when I was unsure. Your encouragement to be courageous and your belief in me power my will to make it happen.

It's unlikely that this book will change the world, but I do know that really important change happens one person to another. Each person has the opportunity to take the same facts, create a different experience, and change the outcome on purpose. Your life is too important to leave to chance or worse yet let someone else to decide what matters. Your impact is too important to leave to chance.

And I know the conversations that led to the book can now continue with others. The message to live the life you wish for, both personally and professionally, REGARDLESS of your age, is relevant and essential.

For me, the conversations about the book have led to some interesting places. And the messages and exercises contained in the book have helped in every case.

From young professionals navigating their lives and careers to seasoned executives considering their next chapter plans, the concept of being grounded has brought new insight.

For C-suite executives focused on talent development and engaging the talent of the millennial generation to entrepreneurial founders worried about how they raise the bar on their organizations and get out of the way without losing control, it has showed a way forward.

For leaders looking to expand their capacity to embrace diversity as a point of difference versus a point of weakness and truly understand the gifts they have to offer to others so they can do the same.

For education leaders worried about reimagining education of our youth and their approach to building skills for the twenty-first century as well as adults focused on intentional development of their skills to stay relevant.

For leaders facing the dynamic marketplace changes and the need for innovation. The work of understanding yourself has never been more essential to lead innovation and change. You need to be fully grounded to lead others, or you risk getting in your own way and stopping the very progress that you're trying to lead. It supports innovation and change for you personally and for others in the organizations you serve.

The work in this book enables powerful conversations to address these real-world conundrums in a way that builds agility to meet the future with open arms. Anything is possible if you believe you have to do the work personally first, and then you can lead others.

And because of that, I have begun work on my next book, titled *Guardians of No Progress*©. It will build on the foundation of this book and focus on what it takes to lead both innovation and change. Building skill here is essential to be your best, and it's in short supply. Can't wait to get started, can't wait to expand the conversation with you.

Until then, I want to say thank you for spending time with this book. I hope it has inspired you to do the work of being grounded, to practice being a student of you everyday, and to lead so others can see what is possible in their life too.

# ABOUT THE AUTHOR

*I*'ve been president, or COO for three businesses and held other executive leadership roles in four businesses. Together, they exposed me to five different industries with sales ranging from $20 to $750 million. The largest included 20,000 employees, seven manufacturing plants, 180 field offices, and 720 retail operations. I've also held board positions for six nonprofit and three for-profit organizations and have received honors from business and educational institutions, including being named "One of the Top 25 Women to Watch in Business" from the *Minneapolis/St. Paul Business Journal.*

I've been asked to share my expertise in leadership, leading change, innovation, and professional development across the nation for a wide range of business and educational audiences, and to reach a global audience via my Lead Your Life blog. My education includes a BA from Gustavus Adolphus College, an MBA from the University of St. Thomas, and numerous certifications, including an Advanced Board Fellowship Certificate from the National Association of Corporate Directors.

What I've just shared with you is what I call the outside story—the factual information that's on my resume or can be found in an online search. Your outside story plays a role in demonstrating your expertise, but it's not the whole story. The inside story matters most, because that's what makes it possible for you to make a genuine, person-to-person connection—and that's where real impact is possible.

I share a lot of my inside story in this book, but here's a brief preview: I grew up in a small rural community in central Minnesota, the oldest of three children. My family had a business that my grandfather started, and it gave me some of my first insights into business and the impact of leadership on the lives of others.

I am a passionate outdoor person. Hanging out on a moto cross track, small game hunting, fishing, water and snow skiing, spending time on the water, making my famous banana cream pie, creating memorable experiences that bring people together, or just taking a walk with the family labs are what brings me great joy. Yes, I am an outdoor cat. And the perfect ending is usually with a glass of wine looking at all the images on my camera and reliving the day. Yes, that is living to me.

I took on many leadership positions in both high school and college, which expanded my viewpoint and accelerated my early development as a leader. This experience also stimulated an interest in joining organizations where I shared a passion for their mission, something that continues to this day.

Through the years, as I got married and had a family, changed jobs, and returned to school, I accumulated many successes, but also faced inevitable roadblocks. More important, too much of my life seemed to be happening to me, rather than something I made happen. It started me on a path of discovering my true self, determining what I wanted from my life and work, and figuring out how to make that happen. And that's what ultimately led to my writing this book. I hope it will help you discover how to create a life with both outside and inside stories that define success for you.